The Social Symbolism of Grief and Mourning

of related interest

The Glass of Heaven
The Faith of the Dramatherapist
Roger Grainger
ISBN 1 85302 284 5

Drama and Healing
The Roots of Drama Therapy
Roger Grainger
ISBN 1 85302 337 X

The Social Symbolism of Grief and Mourning

Roger Grainger

Jessica Kingsley Publishers
London and Philadelphia

First published in the United Kingdom in 1998 by
Jessica Kingsley Publishers Ltd
116 Pentonville Road
London N1 9JB, England
and
1900 Frost Road, Suite 101
Bristol PA 19007, USA.

Copyright 1998 Roger Grainger.

Library of Congress Cataloging in Publication Data
A CIP catalogue record for this book is available from the Library of Congress

British Library Cataloguing in Publication Data
A CIP catalogue record for this book is available from the British Library

Grainger, Roger
The social symbolism of grief and mourning
1.Funeral rites and ceremonies 2.Mourning customs 3.Death – Social aspects
I.Title
393.9

ISBN 1-85302-480-5

Printed and Bound in Great Britain by
Athenaeum Press, Gateshead, Tyne and Wear

Contents

For my parents
and my wife

Introduction

My own field work on the social symbolism of grief and mourning has been limited to the British Isles and the Republic of Ireland. This is up to date, as I am still engaged in carrying it out. However, I have been forced to depend on other people's descriptions of funeral customs and rituals in other parts of the world. Some of the material I have drawn on refers to the situation as it was in a particular part of the world half a century ago or more (Effie Bendann's book, *Death Customs*, for instance, was published in 1930 and *Funeral Customs the World Over* by R.W. Habenstein and W.K. Lamers came out in 1963). It is extremely likely that most of the customs and ceremonies described by Frazer no longer exist, or only take place very rarely. On the other hand, judging by the way funeral customs have persisted in Western Europe and America (parts of the world in which social change has often been most radical), it seems unlikely that they have been entirely forgotten. Where they have lost 'official' status, they will survive as tradition and folklore. Some of the rites first cited by Frazer (1933, originally 1911) are also described by Bendann – and by Habenstein and Lamers, writing more than fifty years later. At the same time, it must be remembered that passages quoted from these authors describe things as they were then, using the present tense, where the influence of Westernised culture would now make it more advisable to use the past.

This is important, of course; but it is in no way essential for the argument of this book that human beings are aware of the need to dispose of the dead in ways that give shape to human experience and that this human need outlives social and economic changes. The urge to perform the 'last rites' in a way that communicates the intentions of the living – and the dead when *they* were living – is present and can be identified even in the most secularised parts of the world, such as Great Britain and Western Europe, the United States and post-Soviet Russia. The ways in which the dead are sent on their way are culture-specific, but the impulse to send them in the *right* way is characteristic of the human species and does not appear to change. Twenty years ago, for instance, no provision was made for newly-born babies who had died to be given a funeral service; certainly, no one had thought of providing a service for the still-born. Perhaps this is one way in which the impulse to make personal sense of things asserts itself in a society which grows more aware of its own fragmentation.

1

The Refusal to Die

In 1969 a book appeared in the USA which generated a good deal of attention; it was reissued later in paperback form and reached a very wide audience. It was called *The Immortalist* and was the work of Alan Harrington, a novelist who had also previously published other studies of a semi-sociological nature. Gore Vidal, the celebrated American novelist, hazarded that it was 'the most important book of our time'. The book was brilliantly written but the main reason for its impact was undoubtedly the argument that it proposed: that man's spiritual self-confidence had grown so rapidly over the last few centuries, and his actual ability to control his environment had increased to such an irresistible extent, that death, the last enemy of all, could now be considered quite straightforwardly as a problem to be solved, instead of being set aside as the unavoidable destiny of all flesh. All science, said Harrington, is a semi-overt attempt to conquer death; all literature a spiritual attempt to transcend it. Following Miguel Unamuno, he regarded every human enterprise, individual and corporate, as an expression of the 'hunger of immortality'. Now, however, this hunger is within reach of being satisfied:

> We will press on, but avoid crabbed fanaticism, hunting down the quarry with exuberance, and above all, relief that our disguised desire has come out into the open. The primary source of our fears, and of all evil and meanness affecting the human spirit, has been acknowledged and publicly identified. It was death all the time and nothing else. What a fabulous liberation not merely to know but to realise that. Anxiety falls away (though fear remains). The main point is that understanding what we fear, we may perhaps act less violently against one another and direct our aggressions against death itself. (Harrington 1973, p.247)

We can see why this book had such an impact. 'Direct our aggressions against death itself' – it certainly seems worth doing if there is any chance of its succeeding; and Harrington assures us that there is. In psychoanalytic terms, what he is suggesting is this: that in the individual psyche, the ego, which is the faculty of conscious choice, should turn its attention 'inside' in order to assert a greater dominance over the destructive and life-denying tendencies of the id, the undifferentiated and unenlightened pleasure principle, which seeks blindly to return the organism to the paradise of the womb, to an unthinking existence without challenge or direction – a life which is, for human beings, simply a kind of death. Against this life-denying principle of consciousness (which Freud identifies as 'Thanatos', the death-principle), the ego must learn to differentiate itself, to know its own strength, to learn the true nature of the battle in which, in the name of Eros, the principle of ongoing life, it is engaged. Eros is used here to mean not simply the desire for instinctual gratification, but the urge to expand, to discover, to flex the muscles of life. Self-love it may be; but it is, says Freud, an enlightened self-love, which lives in the gratification which comes from surmounting barriers and discovering new areas of life. It is certainly instinctual – but it is an instinct for creativeness, not for repose.

This, then, is what Harrington means by directing our aggressions: 'the creative aggressiveness of the ego'. The ego has mastered many problems. Let it now have the courage to address itself properly to this final one, the underlying root problem of existence. If it does so, using the techniques already evolved for environmental mastery and applying itself to the discovery of new ones, then it will succeed. And if it succeeds it will not only increase the quantity of life available to the individual human being, but also improve immeasurably the quality of that life. For the anxieties and fears which men and women inevitably experience in the course of their daily lives are all significant reminders of the over-riding and underlying awareness of mortality, the fact of loss, the phenomenon of deprivation whose typical expression is human dying. Get rid of this death, says Harrington (although he does not use Freudian terms to say it) and these 'little' deaths will lose their characteristic power. The shades of death, in other words, will cease to haunt the affairs of the living.

All the same, it is a shocking suggestion; not offensive, but shocking. All who are affected and influenced to any extent by the religious traditions of the West are immediately reminded of the ancient myths of man's stubborn disobedience – of Prometheus and Pandora, of Lucifer and the Garden of Eden. Whatever man may strive to do, whatever he may *contrive* to do, he should not seek to do away with dying. Death is the landmark he must not remove. It is a gate which may be opened only from the inside.

Besides, we have unfortunate memories. When we have come across this particular quality of pride in human technical achievement, we have been hurt by it, as often as not. Lack of respect for existential landmarks of such magnitude leads to depersonalisation. Machines are preferred to people, in the sense that what machines can be made to do becomes more important than whether or not they should be doing it. People who should, in our opinion, be allowed to die, are kept ignominiously alive. Ignominiously because they themselves want to die. They acknowledge the validity of the claim made upon them. They are kept alive, when they want to die, by people who are afraid of dying themselves. Fear of dying is projected on to them by those who will not face their own private terrors. At least, this is what psychiatrists who are concerned with the state of mind of the dying say – and also, incidentally, the state of mind of the hospital staff who care for them.[1] Those who face death with the greatest degree of equanimity – with the greatest *courage*, because death is always terrifyingly other and is bound to frighten us when we draw near to it in ourselves and other people, however successfully we manage to rationalise our fears – are those for whom dying has a positive significance, a tangible message. Those for whom death is real. It seems to me that there are two kinds of people who fit this description: those for whom death is a real beginning and those for whom it is a real end. Those who believe that God has promised them another life after this one, or who hold some kind of philosophical or metaphysical belief about personal survival; and those who actively and consciously repudiate such beliefs, either because they do not believe in that kind of God or because they do not believe in any God at all. These two kinds of people can afford, sometimes, to think about death, their own and other people's. At first sight, the attitude of the first group seems easier to understand, more reasonable, than that of the second. Surely religious faith is the only real answer to fear of dying. But the experience of doctors and nurses who work in hospitals where there are terminally ill patients, and who are themselves willing to talk about the subject, adds weight to my assertion. The patients who are most distressed are those who have neither faith nor no faith; those who are 'in between'. These are the ones who seem to hold no strong views on the matter; who, if asked about their feelings, make do with some pious or pious-sounding remark, such as 'Well, we've all got to go, some day, haven't we?' and immediately change the subject.

Asked to be more specific, they will become silent or even angry: 'I don't want to think about it'. This is precisely the reason for their emotional and intellectual distress, for the faithful and the faithless are able to think about dying. I do not believe that they are able to avoid fear; but they can think about what it is that frightens them, and this makes a great deal of difference. I would say that this ability to contemplate death, not without fear, but without what you yourself know to be illusion and protective fantasy, is the most important thing of all in our relationship with our own human reality. A clear view of dying is the most vital gift which we can possess. For to acknowledge the presence of death is to appreciate the significance of life.

Which comes first? The courage of dying with which we appreciate life, or the courage of living, in and through which we are able to face death? Perhaps the latter, the condition of spiritual and physical well-being, life lived in the

1   Cf. E. Kubler-Ross (1970) and M. Wilson (1971).

knowledge that it possesses human significance, that the action of living itself is valuable; what Tillich (1952: 13–40 *passim*) calls the 'courage to be'(p.13), a state of soul which is always, I think, religious, in that it relates to a source of meaning outside the immediate situation from which it draws its essential sustenance. But it is possible to know this kind of human fulfilment, to savour this sense of life in the absence of this kind of metaphysical awareness; indeed to discover it in the very action of repudiating the possibility of any kind of transcendent relationship. In effect, this means working backwards from death to life. In the presence of death, life is revealed as meaningless, futile, unfinished, unfinishable. But in a certain kind of awareness, one which is intensely weary of the search for some kind of intrinsic sense in the affairs of men and women, the apprehension of death comes as a relief and a release. There, this man can say – I was right. Life is absurd. The total absurdity of death puts its seal on my actions, ratifies my concessions, authenticates my absurdity, for death is *final* absurdity. 'Death, too,' says Albert Camus, 'has patrician hands, which, while crushing, also liberate'.[2]

We can talk about a scientific conquest of death, but we are really kidding ourselves. The phrase sounds marvellous, but it has no meaning. At least, it has no meaning for *us*. If we eliminate death we eliminate life, we eliminate ourselves. Death is our life in that it is our universal existential context. It is what, in the deepest and most real sense, we are *used to*. It would take us a long time to get used to anything else, and there is every chance that we would be destroyed in the process; that we would find we had destroyed ourselves. Life has meaning because it has an ending. The more aware we are of this fact, the more meaning we can discover in life. If our source of meaning lies elsewhere, if we arrive at satisfactory conclusions with the help of some extrinsic referent, a relationship with another person or persons, divine or human, or an enlightenment which is not congruent with or dependent on our own limited existence, it is still this circumscribed life – *this* life which is in relation with the other. What would we do, where would we be, if we could not say '*this* life'? One thing is certain: we should not be *ourselves!*

There is a universal tendency to attribute a disproportionate significance to comparatively minor losses (compared, that is, with loss of life) because they remind us of the fragility of life itself. Thus there is a definite connection between fear of life and fear of death, in the sense that the sense of life becomes more robust and life itself appears less hazardous and our way through it less like a passage across a minefield, when we have managed to bring ourselves to face the thought of our own death; of the certainty of our own dying. Of it happening to *me*. Once I have realised (Harrington's word) this, I am no longer so invested by

---

2   'Completely turned towards death (taken here as the most obvious absurdity), the absurd man feels, released from everything outside that passionate attention crystallising in him' (1955, p.51).

fears of lesser evils. I now know the reality of what I am up against and can afford to disregard imitations. This applies not only to the inevitable future fact of my own dying, but also to my personal involvement in the death of other people. Those who seek to relieve the distress of the bereaved draw attention to the necessity of encouraging them to talk and think about the person who has died in order to find a way of coming to terms with their grief. With regard to this greatest of personal traumas, it seems that courage to face the future depends on courage to face the past. If this courage is lacking, and to the degree that it is lacking, the present and future will be full of imitation deaths.

To give an example of what I mean by this, it is quite common for a widow who has given every appearance of 'coping well' with the death of a beloved husband, to suffer an extreme emotional disturbance when she has to leave the family home. She was 'prepared for' the first bereavement but not for the second one; for the real death but not for the symbolic dying which followed it. Her preparation was in the nature of a psychological defence, a denial of the reality of what was happening to her and served merely to postpone the full force of her realisation. What would have been accepted as a normal grief reaction now appears as a reactive depression and is treated as such. If this 'treatment' involves any attempt at verbal psychotherapy or supportive counselling, the original hurt may be revealed, and the real process of healing – healing the actual wound of death under the scar tissue of defensive denial – may begin. A woman I talked to after her discharge from hospital following her admission for denial depression told me that her illness started when she received a traumatic shock some months after the death of her beloved husband. She was lying on the bed that she had formerly shared with her husband, when part of the ceiling began to collapse. The house was due for demolition and work had already started on the surrounding property. The event could be explained quite straightforwardly but its symbolic power was irresistible: the roof had fallen in, the fabric of her life was collapsing. Things were beginning to come apart at the seams; she realised at last that she needed help.

What we have here, in fact, is a kind of symbolic death which occurs after a real bereavement and takes us by surprise. The symbolic presentation of truth slips under our guard. We erect defences against the rational, against the normal, considered ways of thinking and reacting, but we have no defence against the irrational – against the kind of knowledge which erupts from our unconscious minds. (I remember seeing a production of *Julius Caesar* in which the audience's attention was distracted at the moment of the assassination by a scream from the corner of the stage. We all immediately looked in that direction, away from Caesar himself, and saw that it was the Soothsayer who had screamed. Relieved, we turned away, back to Caesar himself, and a kind of emotionless reflex saw the assassin's blade slide into his side. It was an unforgettable moment. We knew what was going to happen, for we were all familiar with the play, over-familiar with it, in fact. But we had never experienced the moment like this. We almost felt the knife ourselves. When the curtain fell at the end of the scene we were all very shaken and some of us were in tears.) We shall be much concerned in this study with the power of the symbol to direct emotion and to crystallise meaning and significance; also with 'symbolic deaths' of various kinds. Psychoanalytic theory proposed that every deeply felt experience of loss or deprivation has a more or less direct reference to an infantile experience of ineradicable existential significance, to the child's first moment of conscious separation from the maternal breast or the primal shock of birth itself. Whether we accept this or not, the fact remains that every experience of radical change involves a kind of symbolic dying, as a precondition for achieving a state of affairs which can be considered – can be lived – as authentically *new*. Ontologically, the new must be born out of the ashes of the old, otherwise it is simply the old in a new guise.

The symbolic structure or model which embodies this vital existential truth is the 'rite of passage', the traditional vehicle for the expression and implementation of changes of a deep and permanent nature and a final metaphysical significance. The rite itself is a symbolic mechanism in that it is the performance of a mystery. It proposes an idea of social truth – whether the society concerned is a family, a village, a race or a cosmos – and anchors it into a demonstration of real life. Men and women, young people of both sexes, live for a period within the structure of the rite and are changed by it. *Permanently* changed, because the idea they have absorbed is an idea of the ultimate, of an uncategorisable category of reality which has the power to change lives in an ideal way. They have touched the hem of the garment of divinity, and the power has flowed into them. For such a change to be truthful about the ideal, it must depend on the action of ideality; in other words, upon religious revelation. For it to be authentic as an account of the human state of affairs, it must involve some kind of humanly valid experience of dying-in-order-to-live.

Rites of passage, whether they are ceremonies of social and institutional graduation or religious initiation, necessarily revolve around a genuine psychological death. At some central point in the proceedings, the old state of affairs, the old way of life, the old attitude of mind – the circumstances which obtain outside the idealised world of the rite – must die, so that a new world may be proclaimed. There can be no dissociation within the rite: the change must be lived, it cannot simply be thought about or aspired to. The rules of ritual prevent this. Because human personality resists this kind of radical change with every fibre of its being, it is bound to hurt. Again, from a religious point of view it *must* hurt, because men do not, cannot, grow easily into gods. To use the language of the rite, a divine or semi-divine hero may lead them, a spirit guide or psychopomp may point out the path, but the way is bound to be very hard even if we follow it by participating symbolically in another's ordeal. Passage rites are more explicit, and consequently more dramatic, in some cultures than in others. Such is the quality of the change transmitted by them, that they are never ignored or discounted, either by the individual concerned or the society to which he belongs. As Van Gennep (1965) points out, they provide a salutary experience of dying emotionally which stands people in good stead in the presence of actual physical death. For the religious person, a real, imaginative experience of death has resulted in an enrichment of the soul, and he or she has every reason to believe that the experience will be repeated, that the truth of symbol will prove to be the truth of physical and psychic reality. Corporate rituals, then, are a kind of preparation for death, insofar as they encourage men and women to 'see death in context': they are experiences of 'rewarded dying', in which transcendence is established at the expense of immanence, and what is new and vital arises out of the ashes of what was old and outworn. The whole experience is vital – the death and the rebirth because the scenario articulates them into a continuous experience of meaningful life. In most interpersonal rituals this is an implied dynamism which belongs to the ritual model itself. Only in acknowledged rites of passage is the death proclaimed as real: in social and religious initiations, a real dying-to-rise-again of the individual's personal identity, his soul; in funeral rituals, a real dying of his body, accompanied in most cultures by a time of mortification and testing for his soul. In his commentary on the *Tibetan Book of the Dead*, Jung remarks on the essential nature of such rituals in assuring men and women of the possibility of bringing about real changes in their ways of being and behaving: 'The animal nature of man makes him resist seeing himself as the maker of his circumstances. That is why attempts of this kind were always the object of secret initiations, culminating as a rule in a figurative death which symbolised the total character of this reversal' (quoted in Evans-Wentz 1960, p.xl).

The *Tibetan Book of the Dead* or *Bardo Thodol*, is a notable example of another kind of 'training in dying'. This is instruction of a verbal or literary kind; it does not involve an actual ritual initiation, in the sense of an acted scenario in which the individual 'learns how to die' ritually as a preparation for his physical death at a later date, as in the Egyptian rituals associated with the birth, life, death and regeneration of Osiris and the Eleusinian mysteries of Demeter, both described by Herodotus.[3] Pindar, Empedocles, Pythagoras, Socrates and Plato, as well as St Paul and St John, taught personal immortality; and such books as the Orphic manual, *The Descent into Hades*, the Hindu *Garuda Purana* and the mediaeval Christian treatise *De Arte Moriende*, as well as the Egyptian and Tibetan *Books of the Dead*, Swedenborg's *De Coeli et De Inferno* and Rusca's *Inferno* and other eschatological works (one might even consider Dante's masterpiece to be, at least indirectly, such

3   Cf. Herodotus, 11, p.123; also Lucretius *De Rerum Natura*, iii, pp.843–61.

a work) purport to serve as handbooks to the mysteries of human dying, describing in greater or lesser detail the various stages through which the dead person passes on his journey towards future life.

Some of these guides to the intermediate state between setting out on the after-death journey and arriving at its destination are intended to be read aloud to the dying person before the final departure of his spirit. Some involve the living in preparatory study for the moment of death, and provide opportunity for practise in the skills of survival. In both the *De Arte Moriende* and *Bardo Thodol* the living are urged to prepare in advance for their own death so that their true self, the soul or vital principle, may be strengthened by spiritual exercise.[4] It is quite clear, in fact, that the Tibetan *Bardo Thodol* is an initiatory talisman, one that is to be absorbed by hearing rather than by the process of acting out a story. It is enough to be confronted with the truth. It begins with the words: 'Herein Lieth the Setting Face-to-Face to the Reality in the Intermediate State: the Great Deliverance by Hearing while on the After-Death Plane'. In accordance with Buddhist belief, it is not concerned with the final destination of the soul, as are Christian treatises on this subject. There is no suggestion in Buddhist teaching that 'where the tree fell, there shall it lie'. Buddhism is preoccupied with the notion of movement. The purpose of Christian 'manuals of thanatology', such as *The Book of the Craft of Dying*, and Christian death rituals, such as the Catholic Requiem Mass, is to enable the dead or dying person to complete a journey whose destination is final, to assist him to the place appointed for him by God. The Buddhist intention, however, is precisely the opposite: it is not to help the dead person on, but to show him the way to get *off* – off the ceaseless round of human life, death and rebirth, off the treadmill of *sangsaric* existence in the world of finite experience, the repetitive cycle to which his own *karmic* propensities have bound him – *karma* being the addictive desire to remain human, to rest in an illusory world of phenomena which grows stronger with every reincarnation. The *Bardo Thodol* exists to show a way out of this vicious circle of births. Its symbolic nature permits it to provide a means of escape as well as a description of the conditions

---

4   'Thus, the training in this *bardo* being of particular importance even while living, hold to it, read it, commit it to memory, bear it in mind properly, read it regularly thrice; let the words and the meanings be very clear; it should be so that the words and the meanings will not be forgotten even though a hundred executioners were pursuing thee' (The Tibetan Book of the Dead, p.151). The pupil is assured that even if he does not understand the meaning of what he is reading, it will all be clear to him when he has passed into the Intermediate State which the *Bardo* describes (*Bardo* – 'an uncertain or intermediate stage'; an 'after-death dream-state'), 'for the intellect becometh nine-fold more lucid there'. Cf. also Comper p.37 quoted in Evans-Wentz (1960, p.151) – 'That man that lusteth, and will gladly die well and surely and meritorily, without peril he must take heed visibly and study and learn diligently this craft of dying, and the disposition thereof above said, while he is in heal; and not abide till the death entereth in him.'

for escaping. In Jung's words, it is, 'an initiation process whose purpose is to restore to the soul the Divinity it lost at birth' (quoted in Evans-Wentz 1960 p.xli). It does this by instructing, reminding and exhorting the dead person as to the truth about his condition within the intermediate or boundary state in which, immediately on dying, he finds himself. The purpose of the successive 'settings face to face' is to neutralise the deadly fascination of the gods and goddesses, demons and ghosts which 'dawn upon' the consciousness in this condition by revealing them as '*karmic* personifications of (one's) own propensities, born from having lived and drunken life' (Evans-Wentz 1960 p.133, n.3). 'Thus, by being set face to face in that detailed manner,' says the *Bardo*, 'those who are destined to be liberated will come to recognise the truth; thereby many will attain Liberation'; and Dr Evans-Wentz explains that, 'this Truth is that there is no reality behind any of the Phenomena of the *Bardo* plane, save the illusions stored up in one's own mind as accretions from *sangsaric* (worldly) experiences. Recognition of this automatically gives Liberation' (p.126, n.2).

In other words, the appearances of the *Bardo* plane are not objective presences, but projections of the self. They are to be recognised as such, and taken back into the self, by a process of spiritual reintegration of the individual consciousness with the universal sea of truthful experience which is the 'uncreated state', a process which is like 'the pouring of water into water'. Thus the various appearances which are believed to confront the 'consciousness principle' during its sojourn in the *Bardo* plane represent, in actual fact, a kind of picture show of human error; a terrifying and salutary demonstration of how the unenlightened soul-complex subconsciously views all human experience, translating its supra-individual truth – the truth which is its inheritance and to which it belongs – into every kind of obsessive and threatening image; a gallery of Jungian archetypes, some reassuring, others terrifying, formed out of the supra-personal being of the collective unconscious and set by the individual over and against himself. Thus the self is terrified by itself. The purpose of the *Bardo Thodol* is to advise the individual consciousness that it is baffled, hectored and terrified solely by *itself,* and by the habit of attachment to phenomena, the delight in mental images and self-created pseudo-realities which imprisons us in the human condition, with its successive rounds of rebirths into slavery, and to appearances which grow more and more oppressive as the consciousness is 'whirled round and round in the ocean of *Sangsara*', or earthly experience. In doing this it shows us how we may break the chain of events to which we have fallen victim. Death is not considered to be a 'natural phenomenon' in the modern sense but a victory of hostile powers. Here, of course, the 'hostile powers' are present in the most insidious and dangerous way, within the individual's own psychic awareness. They are the powers of *karma*, of accumulated sinful habit, tending towards the final degradation of the soul.

In the *Bardo Thodol* we have the specifically Buddhist version of 'the refusal to die'. The 'consciousness-principle' is shown here as having a habitual (or *karmic*) predilection for *sangsaric* existence arising from the thirst for life, from the wish to be born (Evans-Wentz, 1960, p.157n). Even though, at the moment of death, the self is brought into the very closest contact with its own fulfilment in the 'clear light of the Void', the condition of total enlightenment, its tendency is to move further and further away from this position, drawn away from Buddhahood by the habits of successive lifetimes, to find itself a new womb and be born within a new body. Thus the initiatory process set forth in the *Bardo Thodol* is in reverse. Instead of proceeding from a condition of limitation to one of fulfilment, as is the case with other initiatory scenarios, the 'consciousness-principle' or 'soul-complex' here is first of all delivered to its goal and then shown as gradually declining or subsiding to the purely natural level of human existence at its most powerless and dependent; the human foetus in the womb wailing to be born, or in this case reborn.

The *Bardo* is in three parts: the *Chikai Bardo*, or '*Bardo* of the Moments of Death'; the *Chonyid Bardo*, or '*Bardo* of the Experiencing of Reality'; and the *Sidpa Bardo*, the *Bardo* dealing with the processes of rebirth. Time and again, at every moment of the soul's sojourn in this intermediate dream-state, the opportunity is offered of the instant release into 'the clear light'. In the final section there is a kind of judgment episode to decide what kind of body the traveller will inhabit in his next earthly life; but the appearances of the *Chonyid Bardo*, the central section, which tells of the 'Dawning of the Peaceful and Wrathful Deities' contains the most testing ordeal of all, for upon the soul's recognition that these are nothing but *karmic* projections of itself 'depends its only real chance of liberation'. In fact, the whole book is regarded as essential to this end: 'The perseverance in the reading of the Great *Bardo Thodol* for 49 days is of the utmost importance. Even if not liberated at one setting face to face, one ought to be liberated at another; this is why so many settings face to face are necessary' (Evans-Wentz 1960, p.183).

Thus it would be true to say that whereas in other cultures the living see the event of dying as a radical break in continuity, a launching out into the unknown, and fear it as such, Buddhists see death as the pledge of an essential continuity. A break in the proceeding, a *caesura* in the unbroken round of existences, is to be welcomed as offering the possibility of deliverance from the hardships and frustrations of life in the world of men and women. But, in fact, it is not welcomed. The central message of the *Bardo*, the reason why it was written at all, is quite clearly the simple unwillingness of man to seek liberation for his soul – or even to accept such liberation when it is offered to him. Souls love bodies. When, because of the happenings of death, soul and body are separated, the latter longs for the former with an intense and passionate desire. Paradoxically, this fundamental archaic understanding, that soul and body belong together, comes across more strongly in Buddhism – and in the *Bardo Thodol* – than in any other faith. Paradoxically, that is, because Buddhism is dedicated to the liberation of the one from the other. But perhaps we may say that Buddhism, of all world religions, is most aware of the strength of this bond because it seeks so determinedly to undo the knot; and that in Buddhism, of all the major religions, the idea of a soul searching for a suitable body to inhabit figures most prominently.[5]

This restless searching for a body has its dangers, however. There is at least a suggestion in the *Bardo* that those who are concerned to seek the security of possessions (and a body is the best example of all) are likely to find themselves reincarnated into the *preta loka*, or 'realm of unhappy ghosts'. This desire to possess, to 'seize and clutch and penetrate' is precisely that very action of *karma* that prevents enlightenment. It is also a desire to know, to obtain intellectual knowledge with which to manipulate the world of things, the inauthentic world of *sangsaric* existence (Evans-Wentz 1960). The intensity of their lust for earthly satisfaction is the very thing that prevents them from obtaining it. *Pretas* are, in fact, souls whose eagerness to enjoy the perquisite of being human has denied them the privilege of rebirth in the human realm and resulted in an age-long banishment to the place of unfulfilled *karmic* desire, the agonised shadow world of ghosts. In order to evade such a destiny, they are quick to seize any opportunity that may present itself to get hold of a body.[6]

The *Bardo Thodol* is particularly interesting to us within the context of our present study because it provides us with a very striking example of a preoccupation which is both very ancient and also very widespread among the various religions and cultures of the world. In Tibet, indeed, it predates Buddhism, being associated in the first place with religious ideas which are even older, notably those belonging to the ancient *Bon* faith. This is the primal notion of the undead, the individual dead person who will not acknowledge that he is, in fact, dead. He will not acknowledge it because he does not himself know it. He needs instruction by the living about the truth of his present state. As Jung says: 'It is a primordial, universal idea that the dead simply continue their earthly existence and do not know that they are disembodied spirits – an archetypical

5   In *Magic, Science and Religion*, Malinowski (1974) describes a more primitive version of the soul's search for a new womb. Among the Trobriand Islanders it is traditionally held that the dead sojourn for a while in *Tuma*, the land of the dead, before turning to the habitations of men to seek rebirth. *Tuma* is a geographical location – an island in the Pacific – and not an alternative psychic dimension, as in the *Bardo*. The soul is thus forced to recross the ocean before creeping into the womb of an unsuspecting woman, who promptly becomes pregnant!

6   *Ibid.*, p.16: 'Tibetans generally object to earth burial, for they believe that when a corpse is interred the spirit of the deceased ... attempts to re-enter it, and that, if the attempt is successful, a vampire results.' The spirit, having managed to commandeer a vehicle, now must find a way of re-fuelling it!

idea which enters into visual manifestation whenever anyone sees a ghost' (Evans-Wentz 1960, p.xv). With particular reference to Tibet, Evans-Wentz comments that, 'in popular belief – as also among the Celtic peoples of Europe – no death is natural, but is always owing to interference by one of the innumerable death demons' (1960, p.xiv, 27). Buddhism itself lends official credence to this archaic idea, elevating it to the position of a principal religious doctrine. For the Buddhist there is no dying. Death is not transcended, as is the case with eschatological religions and creeds which profess the expectation of some kind of resurrection from the dead. It is part of a total ongoing existence in which the two categories, life and death, are stripped of their existentially unique character as ultimate polarity, and become merely alternate phases in the vital current of supra-personal awareness, a sea of life in which life has no teleological significance and the individual wave breaks in an endless succession of deaths.

The attempt to use the conscious powers of the mind in an all-out frontal attack upon dying is to Western religious thought an impious one, for the reasons stated earlier. To Buddhist thinking, however, it is patent nonsense, as death itself, the *karmic* illusion of dying, is the produce of human ingenuity and not its adversary. *Karma* itself is the destructive human habit of stringing impressions together, drawing conclusions from them and acting upon those conclusions as if they had positive value and significance; living one's life according to one's own stubborn interpretation and rearrangement of appearances; believing in the dignity and significance of an operation which could be aptly described as of juggling with phantoms'. Death as an end, as 'total eclipse', as the period which makes either sense or nonsense of the sentence it contains, is simply a concept and nothing more. The full force of this comes across if we say that to a Buddhist death is *manufactured* by human consciousness which exists perpetually in self-induced slavery to its own fears.

Certainly this is a religious doctrine with a good deal of psychological resonance. To the unconscious mind death is never possible in regard to ourselves (Kubler-Ross 1970, p.37); and it is certainly a relief to discover a teaching about ultimate truth which confirms this unconscious knowledge and elevates it to a consciously held existential position.[7] But to people who have equally strong feelings about the reality of the objects they are used to perceiving, to whom the world is a room with real furniture in it, the Buddhist view of dying remains unsatisfactory. The religious reason for this is obvious enough. The Christian doctrine of man asserts the ultimate human significance of things. While existing in an essential relationship with divinity, men and women live in a world which is not a world of appearances which distract them from the truth, but one which

---

7   Cf. Palajale's definition of Yoga: 'the suppression of the transformations of the thinking principle ... the restraint of mental modifications' (*Ibid.*, p.157,n.3).

directs their attention towards that truth; a world in which that truth is incarnated as a sacramental reality established by the action of God Himself.

However, it is at least doubtful whether even this manages really to defeat death. It may accord with our unconscious awareness of immortality, but it does little to allay our conscious fear of dying. At least, there seems no reason why it should prove more successful in that direction than do other religious assurances about personal survival. As Henri Frankfort remarks: 'However gladly man would believe in unhampered re-birth after death, yet the thought of death brings fear…'. There are, 'dangers and uncertainties which no belief about man's future state can overcome' (1948, p.179). Belief in the immortality of the soul, and in its future reincarnation in a resurrection-body, is central to Christianity. In some ways, the Christian doctrine is less 'spiritualised' than the Buddhist, more down to earth in fact. It posits a life, death and resurrection which are real in the sense of being authenticated by divinity. Man's experiences show him what God is like, rather than what He is not like; and death is the most important of these experiences. The human existence of God Himself makes this fact quite plain. For the Christian, the life, death and resurrection of Christ are a true parable of the meaning of existence, a factual drama, whose crucial central scene is a dying. Death is central to Buddhism but its value lies in affording a way of escape from illusion, whereas in Christianity it figures as a vital stage in the unrolling of a wider truth.

Christianity, Judaism and Islam are all religions of violent contrasts – flesh and spirit, God and man, earth and heaven, heaven and hell. Desert faiths, they reflect the harsh contrast of sky and sand, object and metaphor. Their strength is in their undeveloped essence, before the violence of this impact has been softened by any process of 'spiritualisation'. Like the religions of so-called 'primitive' cultures, the miraculous nature of the divine human relationship, the confrontation of men and gods, is – or should be if these religions are to remain true to their real nature – always apparent. Inescapably apparent. The truth of these religions abides in this miraculousness, which when it occurs in its full force erupts into the mind as genuine inspiration, a spiritual breakthrough. What is disclosed in these religions is not a hidden truth, inside the self. Or it is not primarily that. It is specifically truth from elsewhere, finding a response from a source of understanding of which the self has not until now been aware, an unconscious knowledge which responds to an address from outside, from the other. The truth of these religions is the inspirational, *inspiriting*, truth of dialectical oppositions, things over against each other, things in relationship. It is the realism of dialectic, the existential evidence of clashing contrasts resolved by the intervention of divinity. In psychological language, it is the truth of 'creative dissonance'. It is also, and consequently, an experience of the value of the given, which is concerned as a full partner in the vital transaction. Everything that happens in this total relationship between God and the world has positive meaning and, consequently, in the outcome, positive value. Nothing is simply illusory.

These are faiths which are well fitted to take account of the reality of death. Not only its reality as idea, but its realism as a traumatic personal happening, a thing that happens directly to people and relationships, transforming situations, shattering personal universes of feeling and thought and action, They are faiths which deal not solely in symbolism, but in direct statement and historic event, in *theophany*. They meet otherness head-on, achieving divine-human truth through the experience of relationship, the relation of othernesses which to them is truth. They do not see through the appearance to the reality *à la* Plato (and also *à la* Jung, *à la Bardo Thodol*). Instead, they recognise the reality as it presents itself in a confrontation of truths, living in the inspired aftermath of that confrontation, however painful, humanly speaking, such a condition may be.

The rituals of these faiths, especially their funeral rituals, have a special explicitness about them. If they are used to unlock the mysterious gate of death, they may be used by all men. The secret of the combination is open to all. It is a story, not a formula. It is acted out and not simply heard.[8] Their funeral rituals are performed, not merely recited. The corporately held apprehension of the divine nature and intention, the specific doctrine of the divine personhood, which these faiths propose, is spelt out dramatically in the representation of a sacred history, whose purpose is communication, proclamation, celebration. It is not simply a case of reciting a special religious formula and following certain rules for disciplining the natural affections and inclinations of life, thereby learning over the years to train the course of life death-wards by a process of spiritual and psychological detachment. As we said earlier, the purpose of social and religious rites of passage is, in part, to accustom the individual member of a culture to the event of dying. But this is experience of the death trauma itself, a dramatic enactment of a primal death and resurrection, undergone in the present as a way of winning new life for the future – a new social status or an enhanced religious identity. The occasion of these initiation rites is an event of crucial importance within society. Their location is in some public ritual ground belonging to the community; their subject matter a historical event concerning a cast of personages, some human and some divine; their form a dramatic story or scenario in which the meaning of life is played out for all to see. These are things with all the significance of real events, where what happens is underlined by the deepest relational significance and the force of shared emotion, the tide of religious

8   This is not to say that there are no gnostic elements, no hidden or recondite truths in Christianity, Judaism or Islam; these religions also possess their manuals of instruction for the elite, as indeed Tibetan Buddhism has certain ritual actions which are to be performed on behalf of the dead by the survivors (which, however, depend for their efficacy on knowledge of the *Bardo*). But these and other 'people of a book' (i.e. a sacred history) base their beliefs on certain public actions of God on the stage of history.

feeling inseparable from the corporate identity of the particular race or culture. As we said before, this is the quality of religion best equipped to deal with the social and personal realism of death, because it is religion which is willing to take account of the presence of overpowering emotion, of life at its most uncompromisingly raw, of death at its most terrifyingly destructive. Life and death at the crossroads, in fact.[9]

For such an awareness as this, death itself is a sharing, for everything takes place within the context of a salvation history involving an entire community. Death and dying are part of a nation's story, not to be ignored or taken lightly. Indeed, according to anthropologists of religion, religious ideas together compose a kind of corporate self-image, projected outwards in the form of specific religious doctrines and personages in order to constitute a symbol of the corporate identity of a tribe or people, the identity which must find a way of coming to terms with the fact of human death (cf. Durkheim (1961)).

This seems to fit in with the Jungian concept of religious truth as the wisdom of the collective unconscious crystallised in archetypes of great power and significance. The element of corporate, shared experience is stressed very strongly. Religious feeling can sway societies or, according to the Jungian model, occur atypically in individuals as a movement 'upwards' into the individual consciousness. Religion, according to these writers, is really ourselves, but specifically ourselves *together*. When society speaks in unison its pronouncements have religious dignity. Anthropologists have accepted the idea, first put forward by Hegel and developed by Marx, that societies reinforce their own sense of corporate identity by a process of self-authentication, almost of self-congratulation, whereby ideas and feelings originally produced by the social organism are fed back into the structure in the form of moral and religious sanctions in order to fortify it against disruptive tendencies, whether they be forces of individualism and diversification working from within, or natural calamities and wars which happen to human societies from without. The process is one of externalisation, objectivisation and internalisation. Feelings, desires, aspirations on the positive side, and fears, weaknesses, social complexes (in the Freudian sense of the word – irrational, unconscious terrors which originate in the past and subtly influence present behaviour) on the negative side, become

---

9   Henri Frankfort, in *Kingship and the Gods* (1948), makes a comparison between, 'Egypt, where the reality of death was almost denied ... and which in accordance with its static interpretation of the cosmos considered life to be everlasting and paradoxically denied the reality of death' and the harshly realistic religion of Mesopotamia, 'which held that man's inescapable fate was death ... it was known that even the life of nature stood in danger of extinction. And many deities were believed to succumb to it temporarily.' (pp.5, 281). The Christian idea of death comes between these two extremes; cf. Hebrews 15 for a description of the sensation of stepping off the burning sands on to the golden pavement.

dissociated from society itself, and achieve a kind of life of their own. These hopes and fears become *objects*, detached from society but still intensely meaningful for society. They achieve a kind of objective truth, a real presence. Originally created by society, they begin to influence the society that created them. To the religious consciousness, which tends always to think of truth in terms of personal relation (even in Buddhism, where the persons concerned have no objective existence!), these values become a pantheon of divine personalities, or a single divine personality who is able to take account of all of them at once. In this way, it is claimed, society makes use of religious ideas as a means of structuring itself for survival. Negative ideas, ideas of individual inadequacy, of the difference between what is experienced and what is longed for and reached after, are transformed by an immense corporate act of psychological projection, followed by an equally impressive process of identification, into positive feelings attached to life in the presence of divinity. Society invents a metaphysic and then uses it to reassure itself (cf. Berger (1973)).

The primal enemy is of course death. This is the lurking terror underlying all lesser fears. To a Freudian analyst this ponderous sociological account of religion would no doubt seem entirely superfluous. He would find a connection between religious belief and the fear of death in the individual's unconscious assumption of his own immortality: I do not die of my own accord, but I am the victim of some wicked person who wishes to kill me. Religion, trust in a protective father-figure, is my way of defending myself against this person – and I am doubly secure in my choice of ally, having identified the most dangerous person I know, my former rival and present ideal. Both the Durkheimian and the Freudian hypotheses involve a process of wish-fulfilment, either corporate or individual, which seems to me to be an inadequate explanation of the reality of the religious relationship. In the same way, the Jungian understanding of divinity regards as illusory the very characteristic of religious experience which I would hold to be central to the relation of otherness, namely the gap between man and God. To Jung, this division is an obstacle to be overcome, rather than the terms on which the relationship may take place at all.

However, the point here is not whether we find the sociological argument any more convincing than the psychological one; or, indeed, than any other 'scientific' theodicy. The point is that both sociologists and psychologists tend to regard religion as primarily concerned with man's fear of death. While such fear may constitute a limitation of personal growth in an individual, it is actually a source of strength of societies, for the solidarity of the group is increased by the need for security on the part of its members. Fear, in other words, drives men together; the vulnerable individual draws life from the group, whose *esprit de corps* grows in accordance with its sense of mutual dependence. Within the group the individual finds what Tillich calls, 'the courage to be as a part' (1952, pp.93ff). There is no need to push this any farther and to say that this metaphysical security is actually *produced* by the group. It may well be that it is something inherent in human being, something relational that becomes evident within the circumstances of corporate belonging. It is a positive experience of a spiritual kind, nurtured by the quality of enhanced being which is manifested in community.

Whatever religion is, it is primarily and inescapably concerned with relationship. Private religion, restricting itself to a unique responsibility of the individual believer to God, shows an almost inescapable tendency to follow the outline of the primal, infantile, relationship with a punitive other, perhaps because it is in rivalry with the father that the individual child first becomes aware of his own separate and responsible identity. It may be that the developing child seeks refuge within the group and gives it his allegiance as an alternative to this threateningly restrictive relationship, in which approval always seems to depend on a surrender of the self to the other's demands, necessitating a denial of whole areas of the personality which are regarded as unacceptable to the other. In the group, however, the individual receives himself back again. His own experiences are authenticated by the experiences of others, and he finds himself drawing strength from a whole network of meaningful relationships.[10] Rites of passage serve to reassure the individual, that his unique and idiosyncratic personhood is valued as the significant part of a valuable, an acceptable, whole; he lends his strength to a gesture of the corporate soul where meaning is apparent. 'The social ritual', says Berger:

> transforms the individual event into a typical case, just as it transforms individual biography into an episode in the history of society. The individual is seen as being born, living and suffering, and eventually dying as his ancestors have done before him and his children will do after him. As he accepts and inwardly appropriates this view of the matter, he transcends his own individuality as well as the uniqueness, including the unique pain and the unique terrors, of his individual experiences. (1973, p.62)

In *Man and His Symbols*, Jung speaks explicitly about his belief that these passage rites are, indeed, a way of countering an individual's natural and inevitable fear of dying:

> The initiation rite celebrated in the Eleusinian mysteries (the rites of worship of the fertility goddesses Demeter and Persephone) was not considered appropriate merely for those who sought to live life more abundantly: it was also used as a

---

10   Initiation ceremonies have been described as rites which minimise sexual envy and castration anxiety based upon, 'a conflict between man's instinctual desires and the role he wishes to play in society, or which society expects him to fulfil.' The rites are efforts to free oneself from these anxieties (S.T. Kemball in Van Gennep (1965, p.xvi))

preparation for death, as if death also required an initiatory rite of the same kind... Those who have to learn to face death may have to relearn the old message that tells us that death is a mystery for which we must prepare ourselves in the same spirit of submission as we once learned to prepare ourselves for life. (1981, p.148)

Bronislaw Malinowski went even further, attributing religion itself to man's fear of dying: 'Religion saves man from a surrender to death and destruction'(1974, p.49) . In the funeral rites of the Trobriand Islanders among whom he was living he noticed what he called a:

> two-fold contradictory tendency: on the one hand to preserve the body, to keep its form intact, or to retain parts of it; on the other hand to be done with it, to put it out of the way, to annihilate it completely ... into this play of emotional forces, into this supreme dilemma of life and final death, religion steps in, selecting the positive creed, the comforting view, the culturally valuable belief in immortality. (1974, pp.49, 51).

Observing these Kiriwanian mourners, Malinowski noticed how the death of a single member of the community affected the entire people. By setting in motion one part of the instinct of self-preservation it threatened the cohesion and solidarity of the group and upon this depended the organisation of that society, its tradition and finally the whole culture: 'for if primitive man yielded always to the disintegrating impulses of his reaction to death, the continuity of tradition and the existence of material civilization would be made impossible' (p.53).[11] Malinowski regards religion as a kind of social tool, wielded in ritual form by undeveloped societies. As such, it finds its typical expression in mortuary rites. Faced with the threat of destruction embodied in the corpse of one of its members, society consciously chooses the positive option of religious hope by affirming a metaphysical solidarity in the face of private despair and threatened social disintegration.

This corporate determination to consolidate life by taking proper public account of the reality of death, and organising the forces of survival for a massive counter-attack, not of denial but of resurgence and renewal, is extended by the equally realistic way in which Trobrianders regarded the dead themselves, reverencing their dignity and paying the greatest respect to their particular susceptibilities, as well as welcoming them back into the society of the living in great yearly festivals. It was the emotional realism of their approach to death and

---

11   'Religion sets its stamp on the culturally valuable attitude, and enforces it by public enactment' (Malinowski 1974, p.65). Cf. also Otto Rank (1958), who sees the structures of organized religion as bulwarks erected by men against the ever-present fear of death, as this is embodied in the figure of the woman, symbol of natural (as distinct from cultural) genesis.

the honesty of their grieving that impressed Malinowski with the tremendous social importance of primal religion, religion which concerns itself with fundamental matters of living and dying. In such areas of life, emotional realism and psychological honesty may be more useful than intellectual clarity. Whatever may be the judgment of the conscious intelligence, the two opposing truths he describes – the reality of deprivation and loss, and the opposing fact of relationship, relationship powerful enough to penetrate even the barrier of the grave – possess a primitive, iconic resonance which must be accounted for. Emotionally and psychologically the dead live on. Like a man who feels the blood still pulsing through an amputated limb, the bereaved community gives life to the dead, taking life from the dead. But it is a strange kind of life, this living in company with the dead, and needs to be understood for what it is: the timeless life of relationship itself, the immortality of a valuable intention, the continuity of a purpose which is deathless.

2

The Fear of the Dead

Sutton Vane's famous play, *Outward Bound*, written in 1923, is a twentieth-century treatment of an archetypal theme of folklore – the inability of dead people to accept the idea of their being dead. At first. it is suggested, the deceased are actually ignorant of the fact that they are no longer alive. The success of this play, and the fact that it has lingered so long in the memory of those who have read it or seen it performed, is evidence that however hard we may try to dismiss such an idea as being superstitious and 'primitive', it still strikes a chord in our minds. Such works as Swedenborg's *De Coeli* and the *Bardo Thodol*, which occupied our attention in Chapter 1, posit the existence of an intermediate state 'between' life in this world and the final destination of the dead (or, in the Buddhist case, between one karmic existence and another, with the possibility of final release into a state of perfect 'enlightenment'). According to Swedenborg, the first state of man after death resembles his condition in the world, and the dead person has no reason to believe that he has passed into 'the beyond' at all. As in the *Bardo*, there is a proviso in the case of those who as a result of their earthly actions will find themselves either in heaven or in hell immediately upon dying without any pause at all.[1]

---

1   E. Swedenborg (1868) pp.493–7. I cannot find any references in Catholic Christianity to this state of confusion on the part of the newly dead. Information about the 'undead', that is, those who do not know they are dead, in Christian tradition seems to belong mainly to the world of folklore; although, as we shall see, there is a pragmatic assumption in Christianity, as in Hinduism and also Islam, that wandering, homeless, confused ghosts may be laid to rest by the performance of appropriate funeral rituals which are culturally associated with bringing peace to the dead (i.e. the Catholic *Requiem*, the Hindu *Preta Sraddha* and the Moslem *Fatiha*). Catholic Christians are taught that the condition of those who, after dying, find themselves in the intermediate state can be affected by the direct intercession on their behalf of surviving Christians. However, souls in purgatory are believed to be well aware of their own condition, and need support in the shape of intercession and commendation rather than information; they are not 'lost' but bound on a clearly defined journey towards perfection, the beatific vision of God. As Hall (1894) says, 'the manner, the place and the conditions of purgation of souls are unknown to us'. Even vaguer are the traditions about 'limbo', described by Hall as, 'a middle place for heathen people who serve their probation in a

The *Bardo Thodol* deals primarily with a situation of profound ignorance on the part of the newly dead. Its main purpose is simply to inform them of the true facts about their hazardous position 'in between', and so to 'save them from the ambuscades of the dread *Bardo'; but, as it points out, there are always likely to be some who cannot be saved in this way, and are destined to spend at least some time in one hell or other.*

We should not be surprised at this eagerness to 'put the dead right' and make sure that they arrive safely at their destination, wherever this might be. A wandering ghost is a dangerous kind of entity, because he or she might decide to wander *back*. Indeed, as the life on earth is the only real life the ghost has known, it is likely to exert a very powerful attraction; particularly if the ghost has left a beloved family behind, a widow or widower, mother or father, brothers and sisters, who are crying out in anguish for his or her return. We might suppose that it would take a very strong-minded ghost indeed to resist these inducements. For, after all, he is like us.

This would appear to be the crux of the whole matter. The dead are people like ourselves. They are our beloved relatives: the father, mother, husband, wife, daughter or son; they are our neighbours, our colleagues: they are the friend we trusted, the enemy we hated. They can be expected to feel the same way as us. This being so, how can we expect them to be content to keep away, to continue their journeying towards the place appointed for them, the proper place for them to be? Seeing that we ourselves have so much difficulty in contemplating our own death; seeing that, unconsciously, we consider ourselves to be immortal and consciously prefer always to change the subject, our attempts to convince the dead person have a hollow ring to them. We cannot sentence him to death; we cannot, by ourselves, even send him away to paradise. When we try to face the fact that someone else has died, we come up against this existential truth about ourselves – that we have no experience of dying, or at least that the lesson about mortality, so hardly learned, sorely taxes what experience we have, straining our fragile defences against the unknown, our ability to make reassuring sense of things. We could not contemplate death as our own presence – how can we bear it as another's absence?

manner which befits them for at least a natural beatitude'. (This is *Limbus Puerorum*, so called because of the supposed presence in it of myriads of unbaptised babies; a second limbo, *Limbo Patrum*, the limbo of patriarchs, that is, the prophets and others of the Old Testament, was conceived as a place of detention for those, 'whose errors had been those of invincible ignorance and who died in a condition of susceptibility to the light of the gospel' (cf St. Thomas Aquinas (1988) *Summa III,* supplement lxix, pp.4–5; for purgatory, see pp.7–8; also supplement lxx:3 and St Catherine of Genoa *Treatise on Purgatory*). The official teaching concerning the efficacy of intercessions and good works performed on behalf of the dead was formulated at the Council of Florence in 1438–39.)

Herein, of course, lies the very root of our horror of ghosts. They are feared not because of what they are, but because of what they remind us of being. We are frightened of ghosts because we are frightened of dying. That is the first thing to be said about the matter: that ghosts, like corpses, are unwelcome because they are *memento mori*. The rider to it is this: that our own fear of death is projected on to the dead themselves, so that we imagine them as desperately anxious to return to the world we know and love, the world that they knew and loved. And so we make them a gift of our own fear of the dark. A Jungian doctrine of the unconscious would in fact go further than this. Even as in our own unconscious minds we live forever, so the dead for their part cannot die, but live on under the surface of our waking world; always present, seldom acknowledged, occasionally standing forth as the projected image of an unconscious reality.

This may well be one reason for our horror of visitors from behind the grave – that they represent an unconscious awareness of immortality which we have struggled to deny; a knowledge which, through fear, we have attempted to murder. They come to us wearing the grave-clothes that we have forced them to wear. When they erupt into consciousness we are both terrified and affronted, but their immortality overcomes our determination to restrain it. Indeed, that the dead are dead in every way, that they are quite literally no more, is not, in fact, so rational an assessment of the situation, for it represents an irrational determination to fly in the face of psychological evidence which ought not to be discounted and cannot convincingly be rebutted. On an unconscious level, there is a universal awareness of survival, a kind of corporate personal meaning which defies death because it is fundamental and therefore timeless. And this is why those who are vehement about the impossibility of survival seem so often to protest too much. They believe themselves to be rational. In fact they are being neurotic. As for the dead themselves, their supposed unwillingness to give up living may be the very mirror image of our own dread of dying. Their persistence as a presence in our world, either as actual apparitions or as an unseen influence, is evidence of a reality which they do in fact possess, which is more than the mere projection of our fears.

Either doctrine would make sense of the behaviour of bereaved people who are preoccupied by memories and ruminate in fantasies, often even talk to the deceased as if he was still alive. This of course, is familiar to those who try to help the bereaved. Murray Parkes, Elizabeth Kubler-Ross, Geoffrey Gorer and many others have drawn attention to it and it is mentioned in almost every handbook on bereavement counselling.[2] Usually it is considered to be a perfectly normal

---

2   Bowlby has claimed that the roots of the denial of the death of a loved person run very deep indeed, penetrating back to early childhood. He describes three definite stages in the infantile reaction to bereavement: protest, despair and denial (Bowlby 1961, p.317). Acc-

reaction to the loss of someone who was very deeply loved and it is much too widespread to be considered 'pathological' that is, as a sign of an abnormally exaggerated grief reaction. Murray Parkes, in fact, describes it as, 'the commonest means of mitigating the pain of grieving ... the maintenance of a feeling or impression that the dead person is nearby although he may not be seen or heard' (1972, p.57). 'A comforting sense of the persisting presence of the lost husband' was reported by 15 out of 22 widows interviewed by Parkes in an investigation carried out in 1971 (1972, p.58). While perfectly 'normal', such an awareness seem to accompany a sense of loneliness, of social isolation, which was more exaggerated than was usually the case when the bereaved person was surrounded by a family which was sympathetic and supportive and there was plenty of evidence of life going on 'in the background'. Older people who tended to live somewhat 'in the past' were also affected by it, as were those to whom the death came as a shock.

This is, I believe, closely related to a sense of 'unfinishedness', of an inexplicable and unwarranted interruption of normality. Dr Kubler-Ross (1970) remarks that it may be more frequently encountered in the days of war, where the death of a young person occurs elsewhere. We shall be exploring the significance of this kind of bereavement, the experience of death as 'unfinished business', at some length in the next chapter. This continuing sense of the dead person's presence is usually explained as a kind of psychological denial, a way in which the self defends itself against a violently traumatic experience. As such, it represents a benevolent mitigation of reality, a necessary cushioning of a blow which might otherwise prove totally insupportable. It is not a sign of a mental breakdown but a protection against the threat of such a breakdown. Even seemingly irrational behaviour – the scrupulous setting of a customary place at the table; the chair placed reverently for the master of the household who is no longer there to occupy it; the night dress always placed lovingly on the empty pillow – even things like this can help a bereaved person towards eventual adjustment to his or her new condition. Only if this goes on for an unusual length of time, a matter of years or decades, is it to be regarded as a sign of an emotional disturbance in the

-ording to Felix Brown (1961, p.754), 'the fact that the child at the time shows no obvious emotional disturbance is no evidence that he or she is not deeply affected, rather than the reverse'; and Freud himself writes that the mourning struggle, 'is so intense that a turning away from reality ensues, the object being clung to through the medium of a hallucinatory wishful psychosis' (1917, p.253). The argument of Kurt Abraham (1988) and the writers of the object-relations school of post-Freudian psychopathology is that all grieving involves a regression into, 'the infantile depressive state, with the reactivation of emotions originally experienced in connection with certain primal psychological traumas, notably the loss of the security of the womb and banishment from the mother's breast' (Abraham 1988, p.111); emotions which were originally repressed, but show a tendency to re-emerge into consciousness when prompted to do so by similar experiences of deprivation and loss occuring in later life. As Lindemann, Parkes, Hinton and others have pointed out, there is a definite connection between this tendency towards psychological denial and the phenomena associated with bereavement reactions which are 'pathologically extreme'.

medical sense of that phrase. Of course, if such behaviour is seen, as Jung suggests, as acceptance of the continuing presence of the dead rather than simple denial of loss, its healing effect makes even more sense, for it appears now as a modification of the effects of shock by an upsurge of healing awareness from the unconscious mind, to restore the psychic balance of the whole. The temporary suspension of one kind of knowing gives place to a more primary kind. Thus we have an intrapsychic mechanism for facing the event of death which corresponds to the interpsychic one described earlier by Malinowski.

It should perhaps be pointed out here that Jung's position with regard to our unconscious knowledge about death differs considerably from Freud's judgment on the matter. Freud regards the unconscious mind not simply as a repository for repressed fears, but actually as containing elements which are unambiguously destructive:

> some portion of self-destructiveness remains permanently within, until it at length succeeds in doing the individual to death, not perhaps until his libido has been used up or has become fixated in some disadvantageous way. Thus it may, in general, be suspected that the *individual* dies of his internal conflicts, but that the species dies of its unsuccessful struggle against the external world.' (1959, p.8)[3]

It is not quite clear here whether Freud is referring, in the case of the individual, to actual death or to some kind of psychic dying, although the former is, on the whole, more likely, the idea being that the death instinct, *Thanatos*, allies itself with exterior circumstances — for example, disease, old age, war, accidental breakdown of the physical organism — and persuades the person to 'give up the ghost'. Jung, however, takes an altogether more positive and optimistic view of the unconscious:

> We may establish with reasonable certainty that an individual consciousness as it relates to ourselves has come to an end [in death]. But whether this means that the continuity of the psychic process is also interrupted remains doubtful, since the psyche's attachment to the brain can be affirmed with far less certitude today than it could be fifty years ago. (1962, p.412)

Commenting on this passage, the late Dr Jolande Jacobi states that: 'On the contrary, the psyche does not seem to be limited by space and time' (1962, p.9, n.5) The Jungian doctrine of the immortality of the collective psyche is drawn from analysis of the psychological processes of ageing.

> Death is no less important than birth, and like birth it is an inseparable part of life. Here nature itself, if we only understand her properly, takes us into her sheltering arms. The older we grow, the more veiled becomes the outside world, steadily losing in colour, tone and passion, and the more urgently the inner world calls us.

3   By *libido*, Freud signifies the ongoing life instinct — *Eros* as opposed to *Thanatos*.

In aging the individual melts little by little into the collective psyche from which, with a great effort, he emerged as a child.' (1962, p.145).[4]

Freud's view of the unconscious as a kind of demon-haunted attic or cellar goes some way towards explaining why ghosts are objects of horror, why we are terrified and often disgusted by visitations 'from beyond the grave'. Jung's view seems to cast light on the surely more important question as to who these visitors actually are. If, psychologically speaking, all that is lost in the event of human dying is individuality, then it seems conceivable that, under certain circumstances, the ocean of psychic being which Jung calls the 'collective unconscious' might become once more individuated in the form of the dead person, and a deceased personality be momentarily reintegrated within our conscious perception. I am not even vaguely sure how this could in fact happen; the point I am concerned to make is that, according to Jung, the dead person still exists, even if he does so in a nonspecific way. According to Freud, of course, he has completely vanished and his life has been cancelled out. In this respect, Jung 'explains' the *psychic reality* of ghosts better than Freud, although we have no real way of discovering how they manage to leave the realm of dreams and present themselves to our waking minds, in many cases to more than one waking mind at a time.

Freud, and the later students of interpersonal psycho-dynamics, notably H.S. Sullivan and G.H. Mead, regard such manifestations as projections of the self, their only separate reality that of communication; meaningful hallucinations, but hallucinations all the same. Freud's definitive theory of neurosis revolves around the effect upon the conscious mind of psychic material – memories, fears, fantasies – which is experienced as threatening and has been banished to the unconscious. Such repressed material makes its presence felt in the form of complexes, 'sore spots' on the consciousness, thoughts which hurt for no apparent reason, places to avoid. In a certain kind of person, however – someone who has what has become universally known as a 'hysterical personality' – the psychic malaise which comes from secreting highly charged, fissionable existential matter, expresses itself more dramatically in the form of strange fears and compulsions, or behaviour which is seemingly irrational. However, it is only *seemingly* irrational. On one level at least it makes perfect sense. Its function is to deliver a message about a spiritual malaise rooted in an existential nonsense – the nonsense of pretending a way of being that is not one's own, a courageous way of being that one simply cannot sustain. The hysterical neurotic's 'symptoms' are actually cries for aid couched in the clearest language, the sign language of confusion which not only solicits help but signifies what it is that has to be helped, thus demonstrating its own pathology. The help

---

4   Dr Jacobi continues: 'The cycle of human life closes meaningfully and harmoniously; beginning and ending coincide, an event that has been symbolised since time immemorial by the *Oroboros*, the "snake biting its own tail".' (1962, p.145).

such a person craves is nothing less than the recognition of his own unacknowledged self, those aspects of himself which have managed in disguised form to slip past the control exercised by the super-ego. They have not escaped unscathed, however. The price exacted by the censoring consciousness is that they should at least declare their anarchic nature and not pass themselves off as socialised, rational entities. They are fantasies, and must be seen in their true colours.

All the same, their anarchic nature gives them a certain autonomy. They reject the conforming personality which rejected them. They want to be different, to be themselves, to *express* themselves. That is why they are so troublesome. Michael Wilson has described how denied dimensions of our humanity can become demonic in their power to motivate out behaviour and claim our attention (1975, pp.81–84). This idea of dissociated fragments of the self which cause alarm both to the self and to other people was suggested by both Professor Mead and Harry Stack Sullivan, and, more recently, by R.D. Laing. In *Mind, Self and Society*, Professor Mead distinguishes two different 'phases of the self' which he calls the 'I' and the 'me'. The 'me' answers to the organised attitudes of the others which we definitely assume and which determine consequently our own conduct, so far as it is of a self-conscious character (1967, p.209). In other words, it is the objectified state of the 'I', the 'I' as others see me. The 'me' is just as important as the 'I'. Very early on in our development as human beings we acquired the habit of 'seeing ourselves as others see us'. Indeed, it is essential that we should do so, because as people we live only in reference to others. To be human is to live and die in relation. Mother, father, teacher, sibling, colleague, superior, the principle is the same, we fear their disregard and draw courage from their approval. We have the same range of emotions towards those for whom we bear responsibility as we do towards those who are ranged hierarchically above us and to whom we owe obedience or loyalty. As Tillich has said: 'There is no person without encounter with other persons' (in Wilson, 1975, p.14).

Some kinds of encounter are more significant than others, however. Our relationship with our parents is, of course, the most significant of all, as far as the development of our individual personality is concerned; and it is the specific attitude of the parents, initially the mother and later on the father, towards the developing child which determines the quality of this inner relationship of the 'I' and the 'me'. In a perfectly balanced person, which is to say a perfectly mature person – if we may imagine such a being – 'I' and 'me' would coincide, as simply two aspects of the same self. This means that the person I know myself to be would be identical with the person I know others think I am. This, of course, is the ideal of personal integrity; and somewhere along the line something is almost bound to go at least a little wrong. We are led to believe that too indulgent or permissive a parental attitude may result in a dominant 'I', a selfishly inflated ego;

while a threatening attitude on the part of the parents, one that is resentful, unsupportive or over-restrictive, denying the growing child the opportunity to develop his or her sense of autonomy or refusing to make its demands clear while still demanding complete obedience to them, will tend towards an exaggeration of the 'me'-sense, the crypto-paranoid sense of vulnerability in which one feels one is being examined, measured, assessed by others and always found wanting. This latter condition involves the over-sensitive ego, the undernourished 'I', in defensive action of a role-playing kind: 'If I cannot be the kind of person they would like me to be, I shall pretend that I can. I shall pretend to be *someone else!*' The acceptable aspects of the self, the things which I can do or be without giving offence, are split off from the rest of me, which is under perpetual sentence of death, or seems to me to be; and these good bits are set up on their own as a kind of bodyguard, a pseudo-person entrusted with the business of relationship which should be carried on by the whole self. But the self, out of fear, has abdicated its responsibilities in this direction and chosen to live only with itself.

Or at least to try to. The result is what R.D. Laing (1965) has described in *The Divided Self.* If the whole of his being cannot be defended, the individual retracts his lines of defence until he withdraws into a central citadel. He is prepared to write off everything he is except his 'self'. But the tragic paradox is that the more the self is defended in this way, the more it is destroyed. The apparent eventual destruction and dissolution of the self in schizophrenic conditions is accomplished not by external attacks from the enemy (actual or supposed), from without, but by the devastation caused by the inner defensive manoeuvres themselves (Laing 1965, p.77).

What we are mainly concerned with here is not the deprived and decaying 'I' but the inflated 'me', the false-self system so painstakingly constructed to draw the enemies' fire. The main characteristic of this seems to be its nature as a construct. It is simply a construct. It has no life of its own. It is a mask worn by the self – an ingratiating smirk or an aspect of mature authority or just a stiff upper lip. Any life it has it draws, succubus-like, from the person who wears it, channelling his reality in the direction of a lie, commandeering his authority to promote the authenticity of something that is counterfeit. Thus its own life is in fact the life of fear. It is dissociated, projected fear made into the image of courage. Like everything born of fear it is not what it says it is. Before Dr Laing, Harry Stack Sullivan characterised it as the 'not-me' and said that, in terms of its evolution within the human personality, it was very ancient indeed:

> The beginning personifications of *me* are good-*me*, bad-*me* and *not-me*. So far as I can see, in practically every instance of being trained for life, in this or another culture, it is rather inevitable that there shall be this tripartite cleavage in personifications, which have as their central tie ... their relatedness to the growing conception of 'my body' (1953, p.161).

Good-me represents that aspect of the developing self which is 'enhanced by rewarding movements of tenderness' (p.161). It is the me that I usually mean when I am talking about myself. The good or acceptable self. Bad-me, on the other hand, is the anxious self, and is brought into recognisable being (being as an entity recognisable by the self as itself) by the infant's relationship with another person who is able to induce anxiety. At this primal stage in human development this is usually the mother, although it need not necessarily be so. These two aspects of the self, says Sullivan, arise quite straightforwardly from the growing child's inevitable experiences of satisfaction and deprivation as these come to be interpreted in relational terms as reward and punishment.

Not-me, the third 'self', is rather different, however. It is the product of an active, willed process of dissociation. Like the 'I' and the 'me', it concerns the activity of the body; not in this case the body *owned*, either by myself or other people, but the body *disowned*. In other words, it represents attributes of 'my body' transferred to the 'not-me' as part of the universe at large. Sullivan describes the child's developing sense of alienation from certain painful things about himself as, 'a very gradually evolving personification of an always relatively primitive character – that is, made up of poorly grasped aspects of living which will presently be regarded as "dreadful" and which still later will be differentiated into incidents which are attended by awe, horror, loathing or dread'(1953, p.163). It is anxiety which leads to dissociation; and it is dissociation which accounts for a recurring sense of horror, for horror and dread are the experiential qualities assumed by a necessary or truthful emotion which has been refused recognition. It is an intermittent experience and always comes as a surprise. Part of its uncanniness arises from its arbitrary or unexplained nature, for it is experience registered by, incarnated in, another body, another me. I have dissociated myself from it. Consciously I now know nothing about it – but now and again it has its revenge by creeping up on me from behind, when I am not looking. H.S. Sullivan associates awe, the feeling of the presence of uncanny things happening or about to happen, with anxiety. Awe is a kind of dissociated fearfulness; dissociated and personified. It is fear as a presence rather than an attribute. It is, however, a product of the self or rather a product of the self's interaction with others. Like R.D. Laing, he sees a more or less direct connection between the dissociative process, the process by which the self sets itself at a distance and lives in a relationship of dread with its unacknowledged partner, and the psychotic condition we call schizophrenia. In the experiences of schizophrenic people, this sense of an alien presence may take visual and aural shape in actual hallucinations. Schizophrenics are men and women engaged in haunting themselves (see also 'Ego distortion in terms of true and false self' in Winnicott 1965).

If it is true that a disturbed person can 'appear' to himself in this way, and writers of the interpersonal school of psychiatry assure us that it may very well be so, then we are entitled to ask whether the same kind of thing may happen with regard to people who are not easily classified as being medically ill but who have experienced 'seeing a ghost'. Of all uncanny experiences this surely is the most striking; it is an experience of the presence of death in all its otherness, yet presented as an active force, a living threat. It is an invasion of the territory of the living by the forces of entropy, a ghostly absurdity, something which contradicts itself by simply existing a non-relational relationship. *One cannot have a relationship with a ghost*. Fear of death, we should remember, lies at the root of the interpersonal explanation of neurosis: the otherness of other people participates in the total and invincible otherness of death itself, death as non-being, symbolic archetype of all human anxiety. Fearful people, those who are most terrified by the possibility of dying and consequently most prone to anxiety about all the minor deaths, the disappointments, deprivations, slights, the 'expenses of spirit' involved in ordinary living, try to turn away from the challenge of relationship with other people and to have dealings as far as possible only with themselves. In Tillich's words, they 'avoid non-being by avoiding being' (1952, p.71). Perhaps it is not surprising if, in the actual event of bereavement, brought face to face with the reality of death and unable to escape its full implications, they should find themselves confronted not in fact by an absence but a presence, for their own fearful actions in the face of the threat of non-being, of the darker side of otherness, have had the effect of rendering them adept in the art of conjuring. That the face they see is the frightening and horrifying aspect of the dead, and not any comforting or reassuring presence that they have managed to produce, should not surprise us. For this is the face of fear, the manifestation of death in the face of the one who for them has come to symbolise their dominant fear of dying themselves. To this extent, it seems we were right when we said that fear of the dead is the same thing as fear of death. What such 'ontologically insecure' people see when they are confronted by the ghost of someone they have loved is their own fear, presented to themselves, by themselves, in the most convincing disguise available.[5]

All the same, many people have this experience of uncanny dread which is associated with the departed. Many sane people have seen ghosts; people who are not even remotely neurotic report visitations and manifestations of all kinds concerning the dead. I say this with the greatest assurance, without feeling any need to produce statistical evidence. It is just a fact. It applies to people who live in places where seeing ghosts is culturally acceptable, where there is a recognised 'spirit culture', and also to people who belong to cultures where the whole subject is considered to be nonsensical and not worthy of consideration by mature people. In these cultures, where the spirits of the dead are taken into intellectual and emotional account, such visitations from beyond the grave are not so greatly feared as they are in ghost-denying societies. Or at least, they are not feared in the same way. We may remember, for example, the tone of friendliness which characterises the Kiriwanian *milamala* ceremonies described by Malinowski, and many other similar festivals in other places throughout the world (see 1974, pp.171–190). The circumstances under which dead people are encountered, the supposed reason for their return to the realm of the living, obviously plays an important part in determining the quality of the emotion they produce in those they meet. Even in cultures where the dead are at certain times and seasons welcomed back into the society of the living, we find reports of evil, vengeful or marauding visitants. However, there does not seem to be that element of horrified surprise, that extreme degree of horror and repulsion, which seems to characterise our Western hauntings, where alien presences have somehow to break through a barrier of corporate denial. It may be for this very reason that Western ghosts are so unpleasant and so unwelcome; and that, for us, the souls of the dead have taken to themselves all the fearfulness of an awareness that we have not merely repressed but have strenuously denied, because of an extreme of corporate, cultural anxiety. It may be that, even if as individuals we have managed to preserve a precarious sanity, as a culture we have fallen prey to the same condition of hysteria that we

5   'The assumption of roles identified with other personalities is only one mode of reaction to disapproval and anxiety-provoking situations. The other mode is a dissociation of certain components of the personality and their loss of representation in awareness because they are censured by significant persons in the situation ... Even though these components are dissociated they can still be moulded and organised into a dynamic part-system by the forces that have brought about their dissociation from the rest of the self system. It will not be surprising if they, being the produce of unacceptable tendencies from within, become embodied of personified as symbolically evil figures' (Yap 1960 p.129). Dr Yap defines possession as, 'a condition where problem solving processes result in an unusual dramatisation of a certain part of the "me" aspect of the Self, that part being constituted by a forced and urgent identification with another personality believed to be of a transcendental nature' (p.125). People who showed signs of the conditions of personality-dissociation that Dr Yap distinguishes as 'possession', tended to have been in life situations which might be described as *relationally traumatic*, that is, situations of emotional dependency involving a well-defined psychological threat: 'widows and widowers, along with the divorced, and also concubines were overrepresented in our series'(Yap 1960, p.117). Most of Dr Yap's cases were classed by him as 'pseudo psychotic hysteria': 'the possession syndrome was not an intrinsic part of the illness in organic and schizophrenic cases, but only a hysterical overlay' (1960, p.124). Possession, then, need not be considered an actual medical illness. This is also the opinion of Dr Kenneth McAll, who has attempted to deal with cases of possession by means of Christian exorcism, and has had considerable success in removing this particular aspect of the 'demonic-other' from otherwise schizophrenic patients (McAll 1975). There is of course a difference between the phenomenen of possession and fear of ghosts and experiences of haunting. But the same techniques of exorcism, which imply the confrontation of unwanted presences with the explicit command of Christ to leave people and places in peace, have been used with success, it is claimed, for both conditions (cf. McAll 1982, 1989; Richards 1974). Dr Yap reports that out of 66 cases of 'possession' that he investigated in his hospital in Hong Kong, 22 were troubled by the spirits of dead relatives (cf. also Mackarness 1974). See also p.64 and p.119, this volume.

have noticed among neurotic people whom we diagnose as schizoid, haunted or even 'possessed'!

According to Jung (1921), 'ghosts' and 'spirits' are psychic manifestations of a complex arising from the collective conscious. There is no doubt at all that as a society the civilisation of the Western world goes to extreme lengths to deny its own awareness of death. That the kind of mechanised immortality celebrated by Alan Harrington should be considered a reasonable, even an admirable aim for mankind, instead of some kind of nightmare compounded of neurotic anxiety and *hubris*, shows how far we have travelled from the ability to think of ourselves in psychologically realistic terms. We sought release from the implications of our own individual mortality, our *personal* mortality – for it is only in knowledge and acceptance of our vulnerability that we are persons at all – in a mechanistic, scientistic philosophy of corporate invulnerability and social or even racial immortality; and, when the truth breaks through on us, we shudder and go mad. We cannot believe the facts about ourselves. The only death we contemplate is the death of human violence, the motorway pile-up, the nuclear holocaust in which 'we all go together' or death 'by my own wish'. Dying is something we have to decide about. Shall we let it happen or shall we prevent it? This is the basis of our fashionable, schizoid morality. Of the death we cannot control, the accosting hand on our shoulder, we no longer think at all.

The study of the behaviour of bereaved people and parallel investigations into the state of mind of the dying themselves, have revealed the presence of powerful tendencies towards psychological denial. In this, cultural factors have reinforced an inevitable reaction to individual trauma. In the bereaved, denial and repression of memories seem to be connected with feelings of guilt. Again, the subject has been discussed with considerable thoroughness by Lindemann (1944) and after him by Murray Parkes and his associates (1972) as well as by such varied writers as Geoffrey Gorer (1965), C.S. Lewis (1961), Peter Marris (1958), Lily Pincus (1976), and many others, most of whom, in writing about the trauma of bereavement, have drawn special attention to the harmful effect of the persistent repression of guilt feelings concerning the relationship of the bereaved person with the one who has died. In this situation, feelings of anger and resentment are closely associated with feelings of guilt, because of what seems to be an almost automatic assumption that to feel any kind of negative emotion about someone who has died – someone whom we have loved – is not simply disloyal, but is actually a denial of love and, as such, shameful or even wicked – '*De mortuis nil nisi bonum*'. If in fact the bereaved person has any real reason to feel guilty about his or her treatment of, or attitude towards, the dead person – that is, anything that might strike an outsider as being a real reason, a demonstrable example of cruelty or disregard – this superstitious feeling of culpability is compounded so that it becomes magnified. In most people, however, it is simply a case of feeling that 'I might have done more for him', 'if only I'd told her that I loved her more often'. When someone dies suddenly, without any warning or preparation, such a reaction seems almost inevitable; and then it is probably an honest judgment about what appears with the wisdom of hindsight to have been a tragic waste of time on trivial concerns, time which could have been spent in cementing and enjoying a precious relationship. I have found in my own experience of interviewing the bereaved that feelings of guilt and anger are inextricably interwoven, and that the trauma of bereavement leaves a vulnerability, a kind of existential nakedness, which makes these unacceptable emotions even less tolerable to the person experiencing them. The process of bereavement counselling is largely concerned with facilitating the expression of unacceptable feelings and thoughts concerning the dead. It is a helpful process because it allows the bereaved person to renew a real relationship with the dead person, by allowing the dead person to be a real person again and not just a projection of fantasy. Just as a relationship between living persons is authentic only to the extent that it is honest and truthful, so a real relationship between the living and the dead depends on the same willingness to face reality, however painful. (And so, as Elisabeth Kubler-Ross (1970) discovered in her work with the terminally ill, does a relationship between someone who is dying and the people who are to be left behind. The rules of life apply in the presence of death; indeed, they apply more forcibly here than anywhere else.)

Feelings of guilt in the event of a loved person's dying are normal. Their inevitability is brought home to us by the nature of those basic rules of relationship which govern our growth as people and affect the possibility of our personal self-realisation, our identity as relational beings. The psychoanalytic interpretation of the development of individual consciousness can help us in our effort to understand something of the background to these feelings of responsibility which accompany our memories of the dead, the compulsive guiltiness which underlies our awareness of actual shortcomings and omissions. Unconsciously, the same primal understanding of our immortality which stems from the time when we ourselves *were* the world and all the world was an extension of us, suggests our implications in the death of another. In the unconscious mind, the 'undifferentiated ego' holds sway, that self which has not yet distinguished itself from itself and lives only for gratification of desire and satisfaction of instinctual needs. This is the survival force of Eros before it has become distinguished as the directing and distinguishing ego. It does not allow of any idea of limitation, for indeed it cannot think in the accepted meaning of the word; it is prefigurative, pre-ideational and, as such, omnipotent. There is no other, for it absorbs otherness into itself. To itself it is total life. When the awareness of death in the form of the limiting or threatening power of anxiety arrives, it is *controllable* death: death as the other, the enemy without, not yet the insidious presence within. This power of invincible Eros cannot cease to be except as a result of the violence of others. (And, indeed, this is the attitude of young children to death. You do not simply die: you must *be killed*. If you die, it is death that has killed you; death is a wicked person; and this understanding grows out of an earlier stage of psychological development in which the concept of dying has no real meaning at all and dead people are able simply to get up and walk away.)

According to the logic of the invincible Eros, the irresistible force of primal feelings, it follows that if somebody dies it must be ourselves who have killed them, because nothing else has that kind of power. The message of our unconscious is unmistakeable: anger and resentment have resulted in the death of our loved ones. This is, of course, entirely denied by 'common sense' – that is, by our conscious ego – which knows very well that we are not really to blame at all for the fatal accident or the malignant disease. The conflict which ensues between conscious intention (ego-strength) and unconscious drive (libidinal resentment of any checks upon its own satisfaction) produces feelings of moral confusion, the awareness of a deep existential contradiction and the painful absence of psychic integrity – a condition which, Freud would have us believe, is always present to a degree, but which in the event of a loved person's death reaches a crucial intensity.

This, or something very like it, would be the Freudian explanation of the guilt which seems to be the invariable accompaniment of bereavement. In fact, it is a typical case of emotional ambivalence, of the conflict between conscious affection and unconscious resentment. Some of the negative feelings provoked by bereavement are not very well concealed within the unconscious. If they are encouraged to talk about what has happened to them, bereaved people frequently express modified, but open resentment towards the dead; they are not only angry at being left behind, they are angry also because of the strength of their love, which is the cause of their present distress. In other words, there is a conscious ambivalence in their feelings apart from any unconscious anger at being deprived of a source of libidinal satisfaction and, at the same time, their consciously entertained negative feelings make them feel guilty, above and beyond any super-ego shame associated with an unconscious omnipotence to which their loved one has fallen victim,

Freud is quite definite in his repudiation of the suggestion that this ambivalence is in any way symptomatic of an actual illness; it is part of what he calls 'the psychopathology of everyday life' (1914). It is to be distinguished from the decidedly neurotic conditions we have been describing, in which a part of the personality becomes dissociated from the rest of the self and takes on a kind of separate being of its own which in one way or another proceeds to trouble the 'parent self' to the extent of actually seeming to haunt the disturbed personality, troubling his dreams or even, from time to time, seeming to take possession of his consciousness during his waking hours. What Freud suggests is much more 'normal' than this. It is even inevitable. Certainly, in the case of the trauma of personal bereavement, the idea of mixed feelings seems to make a good deal of sense. At this particular crisis in our intellectual and emotional life, we are brought face to face in a very striking way with the mind's ability to feel several contradictory emotions at one and the same time. The experience of bereavement tends to dispose us favourably towards acceptance of the Freudian proposition that within the human psyche the conscious ego maintains a balance between acceptable and unacceptable emotions, aided in this task by the vigilance of the super-ego, which acts as a kind of psychic policeman who keeps a watchful eye on the way we behave – a fatherly eye, no doubt! At such a time we are surprised and even shocked by some of the things we find ourselves thinking and feeling. Yet why do we think and feel – and say – such things? Surely because the shock we have sustained has temporarily disturbed our usually well-adjusted psychological balance so that all kinds of previously unacceptable thoughts and feelings now manage to evade censorship and clamour for attention. In a strange way, perhaps, we are relieved by this holiday from super-ego restriction; but we are still liable to be very deeply shocked and affronted by the things we find ourselves thinking, and even the ways in which we find ourselves behaving.

Shocked and affronted we may be by the way we react to our experience of the emotional reality of death. We should not be surprised, however. For this has never happened before. Not *this* death, the death of *this* person in *these* circumstances. We can never cope with the uniqueness of death, the particularity of this most significant, and yet most elusive, of all happenings. However much practice we may have had in suffering other kinds of loss and bearing other kinds of misfortune; however many minor dyings and pseudo-bereavements may have helped to develop our spiritual muscles – loss of job, of possession or of house and home; failing physical prowess or professional competence; withdrawal of another's love or the cooling down of a relationship of passionate mutual involvement; diminishing social prestige or a growing awareness of personal failure and a sense of having for some reason or other finally and fatally 'missed the boat' – none of these is really *like* the death of a beloved person or the certain knowledge that I am myself going to die, and very soon. Psychological explanations of how and why we feel as we do in the presence of death are all to a degree, a frightening degree, reductions. Just as we have no real, no effectual training for death, so we can draw no analogy which will clarify our experience of it and present no argument which will measure up to its immensity. These things we have been talking of may throw light on a postulated experience of bereavement: death, real death, the thing itself, remains in the darkness. Death is standing on a wild, impossibly desolate shore at night, seeing part of oneself, the *real* part, disappear into the unknown; seeing life itself become a memory. But it is not like that. It is the second movement of Brahms's first piano concerto and the whole of Rachmaninov's tone poem *The Isle of the Dead.* But it is not like this either. The total otherness, the numinous *independence* of death defies psychology. We are all of us aware of this, without being psychotic or hysterical – just as the sanest and most stable individuals living in the most realistic cultures (*emotionally* realistic, that is) have had the uncanny experience of seeing a ghost. We are left with the feeling that our own philosophy comes under the same condemnation as Horatio's. Theories are not enough. We must produce them because we cannot avoid assessing our experiences and weaving them into the web of our own personal meaning, the way we relate to our world, in order to make it our world. Death, however, is the unrelatable experience.

This need not mean that it is an experience which makes no sense, however; it is only that in order to make sense of it we have to expand our own limits, widen our view of what constitutes allowable evidence. We must allow that some experiences can be truthful which lie outside the range of reported, or reportable, happenings. We must; for if death belongs to life – and we have seen that we can only exclude the presence of death from our living experience, our day-to-day experience of being alive, if we are determined to make use of various techniques of psychological denial, corporate or individual – then life must take account of this strange intruder from outside. The presence of death makes life inescapably metaphysical. I mean metaphysical in a religious sense: possessing a quality which can only be considered symbolically, one which defeats our attempts to reduce it to simple homology with anything else. Death is both a part of life and larger than life. Because of this fact all our psychological explanations of the human reaction to death and dying are put in question. Existentially speaking, they come across as valid but insufficient. And the only way death can be experienced is existentially. It is the most factual thing of all, and yet you cannot be literal about it.

This is why, over the ages, men and women have considered the idea of dying poetically rather than propositionally. They have described the fact of death via the medium of stories and plays. The events of a story are factual and realistic, but the story itself possesses a poetical significance. We could describe this by saying that the artistic form imposes its own kind of meaning on otherwise random ideas and events. Art, of course, is the authentic vehicle of metaphysical truth. If we would take metaphysical categories seriously, then we must take art seriously. It must be repeated that our mistake up to now has not been to seek to find meaning in the human experience of death, but to look for the wrong kind of meaning in it. As far as this goes, we have much to learn from less aggressively rationalistic cultures than our own which contrive to assimilate religious beliefs concerning the destiny of man without confusing the issue by wondering too long and seriously about *how*, for example, death can be, say, a breach in a thorn thicket, so that they end up not being able to see any wood at all because of the difficulty of identifying the precise species of tree according to categories laid down in the manual of woodmanship that they possess. Art has this great dignity, that it is the only way of saying some things about life that must be said. Unless they are said, and said often, they will be denied or ignored, and the experience of mankind will be impaired. Mankind's ability to live truthfully, that is, in accordance with the reality of his own experience, will be damaged.

This narrative way of approaching fundamental truths has been frequently misunderstood. Writers who have described the beliefs of those cultures who make use of it have often misunderstood it. They have confused emotions which are incidental to the story of death and resurrection with the over-riding intention of the story itself. The religious story of death begins in sorrow and parting, passes through endurance and testing, and ends in stability and permanence. Sorrow, endurance and fulfilment, both for the person who has died and for the people who mourn him. It is the *whole story* that is important, the entire plot which transmits the religious message of meaning and hope. The mistake of anthropologists such as Frazer and Bendann has been to approach the funeral scenario as if it were a literal, pedestrian account of emotions and ideas concerning the dead, and then to remark on the unexpected nature of some of the emotions expressed and the strangeness of 'primitive' notions about mortality, in comparison with our own enlightened twentieth-century position with regard to death and dying.

The factor in funeral behaviour which has caused most amazement to commentators of the old school has been the apparent ambivalence of the survivors towards members of their own family or tribe who have died. There is obviously a good deal of sorrow, evidenced by the demonstrative behaviour of those members of the family, and often of the tribe as a whole, who indulge their grief loudly and ferociously. A good deal of this ferocity is very often directed towards the dead person himself, and this, *taken by itself*, seems more surprising. Can it be, then, that the living really hated the dead? If so, for what reason? Does the ritualised nature of the proceedings give them an excuse for expressing all sorts of resentments that they have hitherto been forced, for the sake of decency, to keep hidden? Feelings that they have not been really aware about themselves? The kind of thing that we were talking about earlier in this chapter? If so, they certainly seem to be getting things off their chest with a vengeance now they have the chance to do so![6]

6   Vide p.49, The Dismissal Motif. C. Lethbridge (1967, p.58) draws attention to some of the ways the Romano-British endeavoured to prevent ghosts from 'walking', including a method of burying the dead person under a kind of rock shelf along one side of the grave and packing the corpse in place with stones and rubble. In several cases, the heads of skeletons have been removed, seemingly in order to render their owners incapable of finding their way back (this, is seems, was originally a Norse custom). Polson, Brittain and Marshall (1953, p.5) describe the Australian aboriginal custom of breaking the corpse's forearm to liberate

The fact is that funeral rites very commonly contain a powerful element of open rejection of the dead. In *The Fear of the Dead in Primitive Religion*, Frazer (1933) attributes this rejection to a simple terror of dead people.[7] Bendann, writing somewhat later, is quite sure that hatred and fear are the most striking and important characteristics of the funeral behaviour of the Australian tribes she is describing:

> although sorrow may occasionally figure in the [funeral] complex, yet its role is so unimportant that we may eliminate it entirely when considering the specific phase of the problem [of interpreting funeral behaviour] … At first sight, some of these customs might be interesting as marks of devotion, but a more careful study reveals the fact that this is not the case. (1930, p.191)

R.S. Puckle, in *Funeral Customs, Their Origin and Development* (1926), states unequivocally that the funeral behaviour of primitive cultures and former ages reveals nothing more than a deep and persuasive fear of the dead, and a desire to subject them to the living in order to appropriate their specific powers. The almost universal habit of putting food and clothes in the grave of a dead person along with treasured possessions has been interpreted as a last attempt to placate him and so weaken his inevitable intention of returning to plague his survivors. The dead person is assumed to be motivated by all sorts of negative feelings – resentment at having died, jealousy of those who are still alive, anger towards any who may in some way have contributed to his death. Somehow, by hook or by crook, the dead must be kept at arm's length. We must protect ourselves from our

---

the spirit. The practice of piercing the skull to set free the ghost is also very common: among the North Indian Hindus the head is split by hand or allowed to crack open in the fire of cremation, and an opening in the skull is also traditionally required in Tibetan Buddhism. Polson *et al.* (p.107) report that the practice of removing the soft tissues from the bones of the head was customary in prehistoric Europe, and particularly in England and Malta, in order to free the spirit from its fleshy encumbrances. Less violent examples of rejection are even more common; a typical example would be the one given by Maple (1964, p.31), which involved the burning of black beans at the grave side: 'it being common knowledge that no ghost could abide the stink.' A more subtle kind of violence, and one obviously connected with the process of psychological and social denial, is to be recognised in the name-taboos which belong to so many cultures. Bendann gives several examples from Australia (which was her main field of study) which involve a prohibition put upon naming the dead person during the entire mourning period, which may last from 12 to 18 months. The Warramunga have a two-year ban which is binding upon widows, mothers and mothers-in-law; the Narrinyeri do not allow a dead man's name to be spoken aloud before his corpse has decayed: 'it seems to be a universal custom among the Dieri, the Kumai, the Ngarigo, the Theddora, the Kulm, the Kamilaroi, the Wiradjuri (all tribes of S.E. Australia) to speak with reluctance of the dead' (Bendann 1930, p.139). Among the Siberian Chukchee, a surviving infant's name is changed so that its dead mother may not summon it to follow her (Bendann 1930).

7   'The gratitude and affection of the living are strongly linked with anxiety and fear' (p.132).

own kin, our own flesh and blood. They have somehow stopped loving us and are out to get us.

At this point it seems to me that we are, in fact, getting somewhere nearer to the truth. It is assumed that through dying the dead have somehow changed, and changed radically. Their very nature has been transformed, and this is why they can no longer be trusted. They are indelibly marked with the otherness of death and this otherness is so potent that it is able not only to overcome every kind of ordinariness and familiarity but even to neutralise the reality of human relationships and undo the strongly entrenched habits of social conformity. Through having died, friends become objects of such strong suspicion as to be to all practical intents and purposes enemies. The radical nature of this transformation cannot be over-stressed; as we said before, death is something else altogether; we cannot ride it down, our lassoes are not strong enough. You cannot 'corral' death.

The person who has died is *on the other side*. So far as our intellectual boundaries are concerned, he is on the *outside*. Cognitively speaking, to die is to pass beyond the scope of the argument, to break the rules of the game. This is, in the real meaning of the word, an *aweful* idea. What we feel in the presence of death is no neurotic anxiety – unless it belongs, as Tillich (1952) suggests, to the neurosis of simply being human – but an inevitable reaction. It is literally and precisely the reaction produced by the inevitable. It breaks the bonds of the study of man, whether we call this psychology, anthropology or sociology, and delivers us into the realm of religion, of the study of ultimate probability, of theology. The awe we feel in the presence of death is religious awe, and this is the unthinkable and intangible aura which accompanies dead people. It is theology in its most basic and primal form, the *mysterium tremendens*; religion at its most *outré*, the negation of all we are prepared for, or have expected, or can cope with; religion as unaccountable otherness, rendering account to no human intelligence. Attempting to grapple with it, the human imagination is forced into grotesque shapes, which are the result of attempts to project humanness in a mode which is inimical to it, so that we have that degree and quality of horror attaching to ghouls who feed upon corpses and vampires who suck the blood of the living. Entities such as these are potent symbols of an impossible *wrongness*. They reek of trespass, of the wrong kind of being, being which is in the wrong place and at the wrong time.[8] This powerful apprehension of the uncanny which clings to the fact of dying, expressed in our attitude towards the real presence of corpses and graveyards, may, of course, be the same thing as the feeling of dread which symptomatises neurotic anxiety. If it is, then it is that feeling's archetype, and it belongs to an order of truth in no way dependent on the circumscribed disciplines of psychology or psychiatry. An order of truth which is fundamental. The order of truth, in fact. Religion is what social scientists and psychologists call an 'independent variable'. You cannot explain it in terms of anything but itself. Death is the chasm of religion, the shore of the ocean of an unconditioned otherness which can only be approached in theological terms, and only navigated according to the rules of a seamanship which is given not deduced. 'Have you built your ship of death, have you?' D.H. Lawrence's poem repeats a question that men have asked themselves and one another from the beginning of time. The 'ship of death' is what religious people call faith – faith in an overarching meaning, a master-plan which gives man the command over death, a positivity which is able to take account of negativity itself, a truth which is inclusive, and does not deny contradictions but resolves them in a final affirmation. In its critical form, that is, in the presence of death itself, this religious belief has found expression in the developed artistry of funeral rituals. Such rituals are an indispensable part of mankind's technique for surviving death. The 'ship of death' is the rite itself, with faith as steersman and its sail filled by the wind of the revealed purpose of divinity. The rite is an encapsulated religious world-view, a total theology in the shape of a symbolic drama of personal and corporate deliverance. Like religion itself, it comprehends its own negation, because it is essentially a proclamation and re-enactment of the triumph of divine purpose over every enemy, every negative force. This, of course, is why a funeral complex, or group of funeral rites, begins with the expression of sorrow and ends in joy – begins with anger and rejection and ends in acceptance and reintegration – begins with the situation as it is and ends with the portrayal of the wished-for, believed-in, state of the religious vision. Thus it imports some of the reality belonging to the first stage into the ideality of the final one, while feeding back joy from the last stage to relieve the sorrow which precedes it. The shape of the rite binds the individual episodes into a constant whole which has its own quality of living reality, its own truth – the faith of the living men and women who take part in it. Contradictory elements within the funeral behaviour of primitive tribes, and people who are not so primitive, attain an inclusive reference from the meaning of the rite as a whole.

Bearing this in mind, we may perhaps begin to see that the savagery which accompanies many funeral rituals makes a kind of sense when looked at as the expression of a determination that the dead person shall depart on his journey to the world of the dead not solely for the good of the survivors, not even mainly for

8   Cf. Otto (1950, p.29): 'a ghost "allures the fancy" not through any of the positive or conceptual attributes which fancies about ghosts have invented, but because it is a thing which "doesn't really exist at all", the "wholly other", something which has no place in our scheme of reality but belongs to an absolutely different one'. He describes the 'peculiar feeling-element' of 'dread' aroused by the ghost, as 'grue, or grisly horror' (pp. 28,29). Mary Douglas (1966) and others have written at length about what we might call 'the fear of liminality', the horror which attaches to the crossing of symbolic thresholds when these are believed to have some transcendent significance.

this, but for his own good – *for if he does not set off properly he cannot arrive*. The funeral complex as a whole is concerned with the departure of the dead, but it is concerned with this within the context of a religious conviction about the auspicious nature of this particular journey. Because of this, the ploys indulged in to bring about the effective dismissal of the ghost can afford to be dramatically explicit. Somehow, the ghost must be persuaded to leave his old haunts and renounce his former habits, even if it means binding the corpse's eyes or removing its head. After all, having one's head on one's shoulders is a necessary precondition for human life in this world, but not necessarily for the next one. Where he is going, things will be even this different. It has been customary to say that such and such a tribe indulges in such and such a funeral practice 'because they love the dead' or 'out of fear of the dead'. It would be better to say 'in order to acknowledge the unique importance of the event of dying and the passage of the dead'. Funeral rituals contain many symbolic motifs whose over-riding significance concerns the fact of departure from the world of any other kind of human experience. The frontier which divides us from the dead is division itself, from which all frontier-consciousness, all otherness, derives. Those who pass beyond this particular landmark are finally and radically differentiated from the rest of us who remain behind.

The rite's action is regarded as unequivocal, expressing and instituting movement. This is noticeable in all funeral services, but exceptionally striking in the funeral behaviour of culturally unsophisticated societies. Descriptions of funeral rites, such as those given by Frazer, Bendann, Turner and others, contain many striking examples of the motif of dismissal, most noticeable among these being the wounding of the dead person's body (this can be more or less savage, or more or less symbolic); a spoken appeal to the spirit to depart, or the provision of transport and food for the journey (again ranging from the explicit to the symbolic, from actual boats or chariots or slaughtered beasts of burden, to paper animals and toy boats or gestures of departure); attempts to lead the dead in the right direction by confusing them as to the way home to the land of the living once they have departe; the drawing of a ritual line of demarcation between the spheres of life and death; taking a circuitous route to the burial ground, then obliterating all traces of the way followed by the funeral party; following the stately and inevitable course of the setting sun; and reversing the order of normal human behaviour to draw attention to the dislocation of life caused by death and confuse and disorientate the spirit who seeks to resume his former habitual way of life.

A good example, out of many hundreds, of this kind of thing is the funeral of a Koryak Eskimo child described by Jochelson:

After the burning of the child's clothes, the grandfather took a pole and thrust it into the body and exclaimed 'of yonder magpie pricked'. He then imitated the actions of the magpie in the world of the dead with the object of indicating to the deceased that she was passing into another world and must not return to the house. He took some trees from the nearby bushes and placed them round the pole to represent a dense forest. The grandfather went round the pole, first from left to right, then from right to left, to eradicate his tracks and thus prevent the spirit from following. After this, as he slipped away from the place of cremation, drawing a line in the snow, he jumped over it and shook himself. The line represented a river, which separated the village from the place where funeral rites were enacted. (Bendann 1930, p.71)

The difference between the living and the dead is too extreme, too radical, for words alone to express. It is better acted out than described. It is universally embodied in symbols of liberation. Among the Brazilian Kaingang, the bow-string of a dead warrior is severed and his bow chopped in half (Habenstein and Lamers 1963, p.641). The spears of a dead Ba Ila are ceremonially broken on his grave (Shropshire 1938, p.137). In very many cultures 'spirit-exits' are provided to free the imprisoned soul: in Bali a piece of bamboo is inserted in a corpse's mouth for this purpose (Habenstein and Lamers 1963, p.335) while the Mongolians pluck a single hair from the head and the Tonquinese traditionally leave the fastenings of the dead person's clothing undone 'to let the soul fly freely away' (Habenstein and Lamers 1963, p. 89; Puckle 1926, p.25).

In Europe, and especially Germany, Ireland, England, Highland Scotland, Yugoslavia, Poland, Hungary and Rumania, the traditional practice is to throw doors and windows open and to cover the faces of mirrors so that the departing spirit may not be distracted from leaving by the sight of his own image (see Bendann (1936, p.58); cf. Evans (1957); Habenstein and Lamers (1963); Maple (1964); Puckle (1926) and St Clair (1971). Among the Ashanti and the Hottentots holes are made in the walls for the spirit to escape; the Koryaks customarily lift up the corner of their tents, and in Ireland and Mexico part of the thatch roof is removed for the same purpose. In parts of India and Africa and among the Fijians and Malagasi the corpse itself is passed through a special exit which is then bricked up again; traces of this practice are still to be seen in the 'portesi del muerte' of Umbria, and similar doors were once common in Jutland. The Navaho Indians and Banjaras of Khandesh use the ordinary door, but then bar it up and make a new one for the living. A special kind of door is needed for a special kind of journey. The action of piercing a skull, a wall or a roof symbolises by its violence the radical nature of the happening. The formal solemnity of preserving a ceremonial 'spirit-exit' in the family home contributes to the sense of sacredness of the rare occasions on which it is made use of, and also to the feeling of solidarity between the dead and the living. So important a journey requires an exit that is carefully differentiated from the ordinary journeyings of the living as they go in and out about their daily business. As Bendann says, 'From South Africa to the farthest limits of Asia, from the Indian Archipelago to the islands of the Southern Ocean, corpses are carried out by alternative ways than the door' (1930, p.223).

Gestures of dismissal may be kinder and more personal. The wife of a dead Ashanti tribesman follows the funeral procession to the grave, carrying a cooking-pot on her head. At a certain point on the way, she lets the pot fall from her head and shatter on the ground. She turns away and runs back home without looking back. The essential feature of all these practices is the element of dismissal, of departure on an enforced journey, whether the one who is embarking is carried bodily out or allowed to depart in the form of 'spirit' or 'soul' or 'ghost'. At this juncture, the difference between theological approaches makes little difference. Whatever specific doctrine of man or teaching about human essence may be held by the mourners, the message of the rite remains the same.

For ritual is primarily about movement, being itself the type and symbol of significant change. It is only secondarily concerned with the definition of essences, which take the form of commentaries upon, or explanations of, the rite. The message of the rite itself is a message about entrances and exits. In the presence of death, men and women tend to seek refuge in ritual action, perhaps because of the temporary paralysis of their ability to rationalise. This event, above and beyond any other, requires some kind of registering response, some kind of meaningful and significant reaction. Even here – or perhaps here above all – life must somehow be able to assert itself. Where thought and word fail, gesture has somehow to fill the gap. The nurses in the extremely up-to-date general hospital where I worked were in the habit of leaving a dead person for at least an hour before they began to prepare it for its journey to the mortuary. They said that this was a safety precaution, undertaken for the purpose of being quite sure that the dead person was, in fact, quite dead. It was not the real reason, however. This only emerged under some pressure and rather shyly, as if in fear of ridicule. The real reason, said the nurses, was to give the soul time to leave the body. And that, indeed, is the *real* reason.

The Funeral Motif of Dismissal (The Pre-Liminal Phase)

1. Actions performed to free the spirit

   a. *Mutilation of the body to prevent its return*: prehistoric and primitive, Europe and Australia.

   b. *Provision of 'spirit-exits'* in dwellings: Africa, India, East Indies, Fiji, China, Siberia, Ireland, Mexico, Europe. From the corpse itself: N. India, Mongolia, Tibet, Bali, Tonquin.

   c. *Covering of mirrors and pictures* to avoid distracting the departing spirit: Europe, Israel.

d. *Closing the corpse's eyes*: Europe, S. America (Indian).

e. *Pointing the corpse, the cremated ashes or the grave in the right direction, away from the living*: Islam, Christian, Hindu and Zoroastrian cultures; Ceylon, Indonesia, N. American Indian. Bendann (1930, p.213) draws attention to the connection between the final destination of the dead and the mythical location of the race's origin; for example, in the case of Zoroastrians this is by exposure to the sun, the source of all life. Cave burial and inhumation, on the other hand, return us to 'the womb of the earth' (Bendann 1930, p.53).

f. *Invoking the dead to depart*: Christian cultures ('Go forth upon thy journey from this world' etc.), China, some Buddhist cultures. Local and tribal customs: Poland, Britain (W. Ireland, Cornwall, Devon, Yorkshire), W. and E. Africa, N. Australia, E. Indies, N.E. Siberia, Korea, Formosa, Mexico, New Caledonia (vide p.44n, name taboos).

2. Teaching, leading, showing, despatching

a. *Systematic instruction about dying given to the living*: Christian and Buddhist cultures, ancient Egypt.

b. *Spirit guides*: (1) Human and angelic: Classical mythology and Western literature (Charon, Dante, Virgil), Christian and Buddhist psycho-pompi; angelic ministers. (2) Animals and birds: Asia, Central India, Colombia, Assam and Tonquin, E. Africa. The intervention of a saving personage who fulfils an enabling role in the passage of the individual soul to a higher plane of being is characteristic of many religions; for Christians this is Christ, for Hindus, Yama, for Melanesian Kiwi, Sido, and so on.

c. *The dead tended by those who are themselves set at a distance from society*; India, Japan, Fiji. These people appear to be carrying out the socio-religious function of the Biblical scapegoat, dealing in an official way with aspects of life and death which society has structured itself specifically to avoid. An example would be the well-attested tradition of the Welsh 'sin-eaters', who performed the symbolic action of consuming a dish of salt before or at a funeral as a purgative for the dead person's sins. Perhaps this is the social expression of the way in which, according to object-relations theory, individual people deal with relationships which they find psychologically threatening: 'However much he may want to reject [the 'bad objects'] he cannot get away from them. They force themselves upon him. He is accordingly compelled to internalize them in an effort to control them' (Fairbairn 1952, p.67). Here the 'bad objects' are not simply a person's sins but the presence of death itself, which the sin-eater takes into him- or herself on behalf of the community: 'But, in attempting to control them, he is internalizing objects which have wielded power over him in the external world; and these objects retain their prestige for power over him in the inner world'(ibid, p.67). Hence the stigmatisation which is the social form taken by an inner contagion.[9]

3. One way only

a. *The corpse pointed or carried away from human contact.* ('The river, the river only runs one way': Korean funeral chant) England, Scotland, Ireland, Poland.

b. *Funeral processions planned to confuse the ghost and expedite its one-way journey.* England, Ireland, Hungary, Rumania, Australian aboriginal peoples, Solomon Islands, Bali, N. American Indians, Thailand.

c. *The dead person's property destroyed to 'speed the parting guest':* India, Melanesia, Australia, Classical Greece and Rome, Romany peoples.

d. *Tombstones and monuments used to seal off the way back to the land of the living:* ('The durable memento, the paper-weight to pin down the poor soul for ever' (Jones 1967, p.263)). This is a world-wide practice, of course. The custom of ceremonially sprinkling or shovelling earth into the grave is also widespread: England, Sweden, Germany, Russia, and so on. Three handfuls or shovels-ful signifies finality. In Jamaica the corpse is partly covered with earth before being finally buried, 'in case it tries to follow the mourners'.

e. *Explicit gestures of dismissal:* Breaking pots, stopping machinery, shaving heads (i.e. getting rid of hair) etc. etc; all kinds of symbolic gestures of a personal, or occupational, kind are used throughout the world to express severance.

---

9 Cf. Owen (1959). Owen quotes John Aubrey, who describes: 'The living of poor people who were to take upon them the sins of the party deceased. When the corpse was brought out of the house and laid upon the bier, a loaf of bread was brought out and delivered to the sin eater over the corpse, as also a mazard bowl of maple full of beer (which he was to drink up) and a sixpence in money, in consideration of which he took upon him ipso facto all the sins of the defunct and freed him or her from walking after they were dead' (Owen 1959, p.183). Owen doubts the existence of such personages, saying that nobody but Aubrey, who wrote in 1686, and Matthew Moggsidge, writing in 1852, has ever claimed to have witnessed the custom. On the other hand, in a letter to the present writer, the Revd H. Whitman reports a funeral which he himself conducted in Keighley, West Yorkshire, at which a saucer of salt was placed on the corpse's chest. This was in 1933.

4. Transport for the dead

    a. *Ships and boats:* C. and S. America, Melanesia, Sumatra, New Guinea, Tibet, Burma, Assam, Sweden (boat-shaped Iron Age graves, later real ships), Norway, Egypt, Ethiopia. Throughout the world, seas are launched into, rivers are crossed. Water itself has a three-fold symbolism, representing separation, cleansing and renewal. Creation stories involving water originate in Mesopotamia, India, Zoroastrian Persia, Tibet, Australia, Polynesia and America. Catholic Christianity speaks of 'the immaculate womb of the divine font'. In East Anglia (England) folk are believed to die on the outgoing tide and be born on the incoming one.

    b. *Death as a land journey:* Celtic Hallstadt and La Tène cultures in Upper Danube, Austria, Bavaria, Champagne, Bohemia and Sweden.

    c. *Paying the fare:* Around Greece and Rome, Japan, China, England, Poland, Rumania, C. America, Burma, W. Africa ('water, a handkerchief and a bag of gold dust' – Ashanti).

    d. *Propitiatory tokens for dangers to be faced on the way:* Including information about how to survive various postmortem initiatory ordeals: E. Panamanian Islands, Cuna, Trobriand Islands (Christian cultures sometimes provide assistance for preparing for the Resurrection: Ireland, England, Russia, Sweden. Roman Catholics may be buried with their crucifixes, Protestants with their Sunday School Certificate).

    e. *Provision for the journey:* (Food, tools, weapons, works of art, and so on), Europe (Neolithic Beaker Folk, Grimaldians, CroMagnons), Ancient peoples in Sumeria, Babylonia, Egypt, Crete, Greece, China and Japan, Mexico, E.& S. Africa, Mongolia, Mexican Indians, American Gypsies, Poland, Hungary and many, many other places. (The Malakasi Sakalava pour rum on graves; in parts of aboriginal Australia, mourners drip their own blood on to a corpse to strengthen it for eventual resurrection.)

5. Sharing a last meal with the dead

    Ireland, Wales, England (seventeenth century), Bohemia, Prussia, Denmark, Norway, Sweden.

3

The Unburied

In the last two chapters we have been looking at the event of death and the terror it arouses from two different points of view. First, we considered man's attitude with regard to the prospect of his own dying and the almost inevitable emotions aroused by the thought of personal extinction, emotions of anger and fear. From here we moved on a little to discuss, somewhat sketchily and inadequately perhaps, some of the reasons why the living react in the way they characteristically do to the death of other people. At this point anger and fear, present in the reactions of the survivors by a simple process of association, whether or not this actually attains the moral status of genuine fellow-feeling, are joined by very definite feelings of guilt. This attains its most positive form in the desire to do one's best by the dead person and thus to make up for any shortcomings, real or imagined, in the way they were treated when they were alive. Anger, resentment, fear and guilt on the one hand; love, sorrow, generosity on the other, unite with other less obvious emotions and subtler motivations in the general over-riding intention to do our best for the dead. The shattering impact of death, its unique status among happenings, demands the greatest human effort to put things right, to bring order out of an emotional, intellectual, experiential chaos.

We sense, however, that this is likely to need a considerably greater consummation of the power of life, the ability to draw things together, to heal and restore and bless, than can be brought about by unaided human effort, however wholeheartedly it may be applied; and the presence of psychological ambivalence has an unfortunate tendency to detract from its wholeheartedness through the anxiety involved in hiding unwelcome feelings from oneself and other people. Man may do all he can, but if the wound is to be healed it will need a greater power than any he can supply, either alone or with the support of his fellows; it will need the gracious power of God. Thus death and religion always imply each other. Religion suggests dying, either as a symbolic death and rebirth which achieves a new mode of social and personal existence, or as actual physical extinction which is almost invariably seen as the gateway to, or prior necessity for, some kind of transcendent being and belonging. Religion suggests death because of its urgent demand for answers to ontological and teleological questions, questions about the origin and the purpose of living, and because of the sheer necessity, in the presence of total human breakdown, of obtaining some kind of help 'from outside'.

At a deeper and more essential level, however, the presence of death is known to be religious because of an unavoidable intuition about its numinous quality. The identity of death is the identity of otherness. This is not simply an intellectual ploy. The God who confronts us in the crisis of the cessation of human life and the extinction of human purpose is no mere 'god of the gaps', brought in to answer questions which lie, for the time being, outside our cognitive grasp. This God is the God of the questioner, God who withholds His answer, God as intellectual unknowableness. We meet Him in many places, but His presence is most strongly to be felt at the place where knowledge ends and mystery begins. He is the God of the borderline, the frontier between sense and confusion. The ground of all our being, we experience Him most vividly at those times when human being is put in question because a human existence has come to an end. Or at least, these are the times when we are most conscious of His otherness.

The dead person himself is the symbol of this otherness; thus we should not be surprised that the corpse is the centre of all kinds of ritual actions which are designed to safeguard it from contamination by profane objects or people. The facts of physical decay and the danger from disease, as well as the natural distaste we feel at an object which was once a person, have led us to assume that the awe which surrounds a corpse is wholly an expression of disgust, when in fact it is an acknowledgment of holiness. Indeed, such taboos are invariably a sign of the sacred labels attached to persons, places and things which are perceived to belong to God and not to man.[1] The dead person belongs to God; the taboo quality of his corpse is the symbol of his new status.

This being so, it is at least likely that a good deal of the fear of the dead we were talking about in the last chapter is, in fact, 'liminal awe', the forbidden, untouchable quality assumed by someone who has finally left the human realm and entered the territory of divinity. After all, it is an established psychological principle that forbidden subjects become actively disgusting in accordance with the severity of the sanctions surrounding their discussion, and that this happens regardless of the original reason for their being banned. In this way the ego defends itself against temptation, by making the disturbing and initially harmful into the positively loathsome.[2]

1   Cf. Douglas (1966).
2   This seems to cast some light on the attitude towards sexual expression in the monastically orientated Christianity of the early Middle Ages.

The presence of holiness involves a suspension of ordinary activities and normal attitudes. If the event of death, the awesome frontier of mortality, is a holy event, we should expect to find that normal procedures give way before it. This will happen not simply as a natural reaction to shock, the traumatic effect of the unexpected and emotionally devastating, but as a means of making a definite point and transmitting a particular message. It will happen in a contrived and purposeful way. If funeral rituals are to be authentic – that is, if they are to be true to the states of mind which they attempt to express – then they must take account of the extreme confusion of bereavement. At some stage in their organisation they must inform us, clearly and unmistakedly, 'that the time is out of joint'. They must be organised to do this. There must be wrongness and outrage, or at least its inescapable suggestion; so that what is presented to heaven is the confession of existential reality, the human truth of the situation, which is a world from which all order and rightness have been raped by a happening of quite monumental wrongness. No wonder, then, that the religious awe involved in the confrontation with the unknown is so strongly tinged with anger and resentment.

The evidence of funeral wakes throughout the world seems to suggest that those who assist at a death are extremely conscious of the element of the unknown and unknowable which lies ahead. They themselves, of course, face a time of emptiness and confusion, of searching for an elusive presence, a liminal period of emotional chaos, which is the very mirror image of the situation which they believe the dead themselves to be entering. They are doing a kindness to the dead person by starting him off on his journey; they do not hate him; indeed, they are appalled at the idea that he might, through their own carelessness or neglect, be deprived of the chance of making this essential journey. Neither do they fear him, for they are only afraid of the anger of those dead people who are denied an adequate funeral and so find themselves frustrated in their attempts to be properly dead. But being properly dead involves, to begin with, being plunged into an unavoidable state of liminal chaos, a state which is both holy, as purgatory is holy, and formless, as limbo is the perfect symbol of formlessness. A place which is not really a place, only a memory and a potentiality, hopeless as in limbo, hopeful as in purgatory. A twilight zone between existences, rather than an existence in itself.

This is the rite's central section, the time of violent testing and personal disintegration, of striking reversals and meaningless juxtapositions; meaningless, that is, outside the context of the rite which contains them. Because it is the central moment of change, the 'inbetween' time of dissolution and rebirth, it is central to all passage rites, and not only funerals. However, in funerals it is most strikingly vivid and dramatic, for the otherness of death is the most dramatic otherness of all and its ritual expression the holiest.[3]

The ritual complex begins in a definite movement of dismissal and ends in a gesture of acceptance and reintegration. In this, the central section, formlessness reigns supreme and the guidelines of behaviour are cut. This fact is demonstrated most vividly by the number and frequency of examples of the reversal of everyday practice, departures from living custom, which are both prescriptive and descriptive, ordering the ghost to move in one direction and one direction only, and symbolising the existential chaos in which his necessary journeying involves his survivors, the turmoil and disorganisation which he leaves behind, the human wrongness which is the other side of the coin to the rightness of the divine demand.

3   Examples of what we should describe as 'chaotic' funeral behaviour cover many different kinds of activity. The most notable of these is, of course, the wake. Habenstein and Lamers provide a functionalist explanation: 'It seems worlds apart from the main purpose that mourning ceremonies should sometimes degenerate into eating and drinking bouts, or sports tournaments; or should be marked by dancing and gay music, drinking, carousing and storytelling. But one must remember that social instinct too is powerful, and that mourners can be divided roughly into two groups, those whose grief for the dead prevents them from enjoying themselves, and those whose grief does not so prevent them – for the latter to come together is to provide the first essential for sociability' (1963, p.769). However, it is impossible to get away from the fact that such behaviour is still wholly inappropriate if it is no more than thoughtless conviviality. Some cultures have restrained wakes and subdued post-funeral meals. Habenstein and Lamers give examples from Sweden, Ethiopia, El Salvador, Panama, Ecuador and Guatemala, and the Mormon and Amish cults of North America (pp. 288, 409, 599, 603, 608, 648, 716, 719). In other places, however, the period following the initial rite of dismissal is marked by behaviour which is demonstrative, and even violent, and which appears as a striking expression of a state of affairs in which everything 'normal', 'reasonable' and 'civilised' has been rendered inappropriate by the implosion of events and categories with which human beings cannot cope: with which they ought not to be able to cope, because they are characteristic of the humanly opaque aspect of divinity. Thus even the outrageous activities described in O'Suilleabhain's *Irish Wake Amusements*, the horse-play, sadism and overt profanity, fall within the scope of the rite, as do the mock battles of Egyptian royal funerals and the more joyous customs of Rumania, Italy, the Ukraine, Mexico and the islands of the Pacific Ocean, the week-long wakes of Laos and the dual wake-feast of the Ashanti (O'Suilleabhain (1967, pp.23, 159, 160); Habenstein and Lamers (1963, pp.105, 223)). Habenstein and Lamers describe similar festivities among the Fanti, the Balinese, the Azande, the Menabe and Ikongo of Madagascar, and in the Philippines, Dahomey and Papua, Czarist Russia, Poland, Hungary, rural Brazil, Guatemala, Mexico and pre-Communist China (pp. 222, 226, 251, 280, 291, 307, 340, 356, 428, 590, 595, 648, 725). Jones describes riotous funeral behaviour in Kafiristan (1967, p.48); Shropshire among the Southern Bantu (1938, p.137) and Polson *et al.* in Estonia (1953, p.8). On the other hand, the ritualised wailing and self-wounding which traditionally takes place at funerals among the Coptic Christians of Ethiopia, in the Philippine Islands and Melanesia (Habenstein and Lamers 1963, pp.203, 355; Bendann 1930, p.8) and also in Yugoslavia and Poland (Habenstein and Lamers, pp.446, 484), and among the Dakota and Jivaro Indians of North America, also contribute to the image of social and personal breakdown, of total existential chaos, which the rite attempts both to transmit and contain – or rather to contain by transmitting in the context of a meaningful declaration about life *as a whole*.

The presence of chaos demands at least the promise of unity. The idea of wholeness is also symbolically present in the rite's central section, side by side with all the evidence of anarchy and disruption, as the living and the dead join forces in order to face a testing ordeal, whose purpose is the reconstruction of a viable universe of corporate experience. This ordeal represents confusion and chaos for the mourners, and purgatorial purification, a reshaping of essential being, for the dead themselves. The connection between the process whereby the living are reborn into a new human status, and the one which initiates the dead into their new life beyond the grave, is very close. At its most basic level, indeed, it is identical. What is involved is an essential change. The uniqueness of the event accounts for both its holiness and its universal scope, as its implications spread out in a widening circle to include even those who are not directly concerned, but find themselves, in the language of John Donne, diminished by it. 'Whatever is dealt at her funeral today, shall be dealt tomorrow at mine.'[4] One thing at least is clear. The conflict, confusion and violence of the wake are not accidental; they are what the wake is about. They are the message of the rite's central section. The wake expresses the quality of reality at this particular time. In fact, it transmits many contradictory messages – joy, sorrow, division, respect, love, hatred, confidence, resentment, anger, guilt and fear – which together add up to one unmistakably clear signal about the confusion and shattering of norms, which in itself signifies the collapse of a universe. This confusion and collapse is presented as a direct contrast to the order which preceded it and the unity which is promised for the future. Because it is part of the special ritual complex which is used to symbolise human dying, the wake, and all the other examples of anarchic, abnormal and unexpected behaviour which are associated with it, is able to make this particular statement about the quality of the present moment with unique power and effectiveness.

It is important to stress the fact that the ceremonies with which a society greets the death of one of its members, though they may resemble unconscious patterns in the individual's mode of organisation, are not to be simply identified with those patterns. What we have here is not the socially sanctioned catharsis of individual anxiety, but something entirely different. This difference is not mainly one of quantity – many people finding relief from the unconscious pressures of the love–hate syndrome – but of quality. The ambivalence expressed in the wake is not a symptom, not even a symptom which special circumstances have revealed as the outward sign of a malady; it is a proclamation, a conscious message. It is not concerned with past feelings and attitudes but with the state of affairs in the present. The chaos of the wake is a public statement made about the present state, not of the individual, but of the world. The wake is society's way of saying that the

4   Irish wake verse, c. 1810 (O'Suilleabhain 1967, p.18).

world has changed out of all recognition. The world of the mourners is publicly shattered. For them, things are finally and irretrievably changed. 'Things fall apart, the centre cannot hold' (Yeats). Even given the possibility that somehow the world may be re-made, it will never be the same again. And for the present, the evident, publicly proclaimed truth is that of anarchy and chaos.

O'Suilleabhain regards the festivities as a way of 'playing down' the importance of death by disguising the radical and irreversible nature of what has happened: 'Both relatives and friends strove to show that Death was but a trivial occurrence, which could be alleviated by all the features of the wake: the feasting and drinking, the attendance at the wake-house, the fun and amusements, even the keening.' The purpose is to 'assure [the deceased] of his popularity and of his continuing presence as one of the company'(1967, p.172). Again, this accounts for some of the features of some wakes; but what of those occasions when the corpse was treated with disrespect or even abuse? It is surely not really very satisfactory to discount these exceptions to the rule of respect and affection by saying that they proceeded from ignorance of the wake's original purpose, which had become 'blurred by the passage of time'. The motive of reassurance is certainly present, as the mourners proclaim their solidarity with the dead person; but surely their main intention is not to safeguard *themselves*, so much as to protect *him* in his time of trial, and to give him the benefit of their company in this terrifying new state that he has entered. Other motives – principally the desire to launch him finally on his way, to make sure that he accepts the facts about what has happened to him so that he, and they, may finally rest in peace – provide a continual counterpoint to this primary intention, and the resulting confusion is a powerful presentation of the truth we have distinguished above, the truth of chaos.

The dominant motif of the Irish wake is, after all, that of conflict. Despite the author's attempt to stress the merry and festive nature of the proceedings, O'Suilleabhain's book reveals that, far from being an unfortunate exception to the rule, violence is the fundamental factor involved. The wake is most itself when it is most violent. It is not very surprising, perhaps, that death should be a recurrent motif in the games played on such an occasion; but this is death in its most violent form, not a peaceful 'passing over', but death the result of conflict and the occasion of trials and testings, death as an ordeal. Ordeals and conflicts figured frequently in the class of imitative games described in *Irish Wake Amusements*, and we are told of mock battles, mock trials, mock deaths, mock corpses. There are games called 'Lifting the Corpse' (p.39), 'Fair Judge and Foul Judge' (p.51) and 'Mock Court' (p.75). Other games appear to concentrate on a player's being compelled to make a journey from one place to another through various dangers, or to perform some apparently simple task which the other players succeed in making as difficult and painful as possible. A notable example of this is 'Stealing the Goats from Hell' (p.42); another is the game called 'Cutting the Timber' (p.82), in which a man lay down across the threshold of the kitchen (ostensibly representing a saw) and was dragged backwards and forwards by his companions, some of whom held his head and shoulders and the others his feet, until one or the other side won and he finally crossed over the threshold or was dragged back completely into the room. The theme of entry into and exit from a room is repeated in 'Selling the Colts' (p.84), in which players were driven into the kitchen to be subjected to various indignities, all allegedly germane to the marketing and subsequent branding of livestock ('mud or dirty water was used unsparingly for this purpose'): 'arguments and fighting would then break out on both sides, and the animals did little to lessen the tumult'. Violence offered to the corpse itself seems to have been incidental to the general riotousness of the proceedings as a whole. O'Suilleabhain claims that generally speaking the corpse was only allowed to suffer indignity when it became involved through the pranks of the many mischief-makers who were always present at the wakes. That it should ever have happened at all is surely strong evidence of social acceptance of the wake as a time of licence and the respect with which lawlessness was regarded on these occasions! One thing stands out from the confusion. To try and understand the particular significance of, or reason for, each individual action, or to ask why mourners should be joyful or derisive or resentful, and how, if they are one of these things, they can also and at the same time be all the others, is to miss the point. The wake does not explain anything. It presents something. It provides a safe (in the sense of socially acceptable) framework for the free expression of emotion, any emotions. In fact the more varied the emotions represented, the better from the point of view of the wake, for its business is to show the difference between the world as it was when the dead person was alive – ordered, controlled, above all normal – and the way it is now.

The fact is that the wake is inexplicable *on purpose*, in order to make a dramatic point about inexplicability. Like the drama, the rite contrives to isolate the present moment by allowing us to withdraw for a time from our preoccupation with past and future, and the flux of change by which past and future merge within our consciousness, and enter into a symbolic present which is made available to us by the action of setting it at a distance, placing it temporarily 'outside' time. The rite shares with the theatre the quality of presentness, a kind of unity and directness which comes from taking one principal idea, one main point, and bringing us face to face with it in a living encounter. The purpose of both is impact rather than interpretation. The play's immediate effect governs all reflection upon it; the interpretation of single events or ideas within the drama waits upon our assessment of the action as a whole, and this draws its force from our experience of the play *in situ*, that is, as we are immediately involved in it as actors or spectators.

Theatre and ritual work by direct impression, unmediated encounter, living relations. The play is not the novel, nor the rite the sermon.

O'Suilleabhain concentrates on the wake as a form of entertainment. This is not only because it is sometimes dramatic and often hilarious; principally it is because it is staged. It is the theatrical nature of its competitions and games, their imitative quality, which allows those taking part to benefit psychologically from it in the same way that they would benefit from a visit to the theatre – the right kind of theatre, homely and permissive, and the right kind of play, emotional, uninhibited and sentimental. All sorts of feelings which emerge in the theatre do so at the wake; an awareness of belonging and solidarity, of membership of the family of mankind, and the closer and more personal membership of a particular community; the cathartic release of emotion which belongs to the action of identifying with another person, or group of people, in a moment of crisis or suffering; the general relaxation of anxieties and of inhibitions which the sharing of a fantasy world allows. In this way, all the emotions which accompany loss – anger, despair, resentment and the awful feeling of frustration – are encouraged by the crude theatrical mechanism of the wake to contribute to its primary purpose, the establishment of the one clear and unmistakable message about chaos, now appreciable in human terms, as a human experience.

Thus the wake becomes a kind of exaltation of unruliness. Writing in 1853, J.G.A. Prim complains that, 'it is difficult to obtain precise details about the wake games because of their apparent obscurity'. He is quick to point out, however, that the obscurity was not indulged in for its own sake, for 'the peasantry had no idea of outraging propriety or religion in their performance, holding an unquestioned faith that such observances were right and proper at wakes, whilst under any other circumstances they would shrink with horror from such indelicate exhibition' (1853, p.334). The obscurity and perversity related to the rite, and were only to be regarded within the context of the rite as a whole. Prim describes a game in which a mimed priest, representative of all the forces of rationality and propriety, enters into the conflict with the master of the wake, a personage known as the *borekeen*, and is first of all thoroughly discomfited and then finally expelled from the room. In, 'Drawing the Ship out of the Mud', 'the men actually presented themselves before the rest of the assembly, females as well as males, in a state of nudity'; in another favourite game the women performers dressed up as men and proceeded to 'conduct themselves in a very strange manner'(1853, p.334). We have descriptions of similar occurrences at African wakes, in which the female members of a tribe assume the dominant role in the proceedings and behave with an unaccustomed lewdness, wearing men's clothes as a part of the general reversal of normal behaviour.

There seems little doubt that this kind of behaviour is reactive in the sense that it comes from too great a preoccupation with order and propriety, not too little.

The wake is a protest against an unattainable ordinariness, a public normality, a world which demands acceptance and submission but can no longer support these things; a world which says to the dispossessed 'come, forget, build yourself a new home', but continues to withhold the building materials. Among the Ndembu, according to Turner:

> a multiplicity of conflict situations is correlated with a high frequency of ritual performances ... instead of coming against one another in the blind antagonism of material interest [opposing social principles] are reinstituted against one another in the transcendent, conscious, recognizant unity of Ndembu society whose principles they are. And so, in a sense, they actually *become* a play of forces instead of a bitter battle. (1974, pp.10, 71)

He calls this special kind of sharing – reconciliation within the structure of the rite – *communitás*. As in the 'rituals of rebellion' described by Max Gluckman, wake violence comes first of all from a desire for obedience and conformity which cannot be satisfied. Gluckman maintains that the purpose of such licensed outbreaks of violence and rebellion is in fact to take nonconformity and dissent 'into the system' by giving it the kind of social recognition afforded by all corporate rituals. 'Such rituals of rebellion, by canalising social tensions, perpetuate the established systems of political organisations' (1954, p.24).

Describing wakes as they take place today in Southern Ireland, Kevin Toulis says that: 'In the face of the terrifying and the irrational, the loss of a parent, a spouse or a child, and the possibility of our own death, public death rites provide both a space for 'irrational' grief to be acted out, and a structure to reintegrate mourners back into society' (1995, p.20). The wake, by exalting unruliness and perversity, contrives to establish the primacy of the social order and stability which is sufficiently sure of itself to allow its opposite to be temporarily exalted. The very fact of public ritual asserts social order; whatever the individual rite says, it says within the context of, and in relation to, the established fact of social belonging.

Thus hilarity may, within the context of the rite, be an expression of grief, and unruliness the homage paid to restraint. In this way art protects the truth of emotion and contains its consequences by giving form to its aspirations; real symbolic form which has the effect of inspiriting, transforming, renewing. The rite, like the theatre which it resembles, employs its villains *in order* to create its heroes, realises its defeats to achieve its victories. The rite, like the theatre, is a way of showing everything that happens and everything that *can* happen. Its outward appearance may be crude, its performance inept, its attempts at depicting reality naive, but its identity as symbol gives it an infinite resonance. 'Inside' the articulated drama of human and divine truth presented by the funeral ritual there is a picture of chaos, a representation of disruption, the no-man's land between life and death, between the human and divine realms, characterised by the awesome holiness which belongs to the latter and the incompleteness and comparative inadequacy and imperfection of the former. A *negative* period characterised by absences rather than presences, where divinity is apprehended in its awesome aspect, as the prospect of judgment and vengeance for duties unperformed and sins committed, and humanity known only as a remembered viability, totally lost, irrevocably surrendered, but still longed for, still enjoyed in fantasy; an ocean of becoming, in which the traveller must either sink or swim, a place which is neither earth nor heaven nor hell; a place which is no-place, and consequently neither easy to get into or to escape from.

This central movement of the rite gives rise to images which we recognise from the mythology of religion – the perilous *Bardo* appearance of an illusory and dangerous reality, purgatory, the limbo of Christian mythology, the dark side of otherness. It reveals itself as a place of ordeals, of the most agonising experiences which reach through to the traveller's innermost being, so that every particle of his former existence is painfully neutralised and purged away, without his ever actually dying and finding peace; as a life which is no-life, amid things which have meaning and no existence, shapes and forms of an intolerable relevance which provide no human satisfaction, no known landmark of familiar experience or place to rest. The land of not yet and perhaps not ever; the land of neither nor; the land of ghosts.

The idea of an in-between state which is difficult both to get into and to get out of is suggested by the funeral behaviour of many peoples, both ancient and modern. It belongs of course to the understanding of death as a perilous journey; and this again reflects the religious idea of dying as an initiation, a process involving the pain of self-transcendence, the elimination of the old way of being in preparation for life of a radically different kind. Mythology tells of difficult voyages undertaken by heroes into the land of the dead, perilous tasks undertaken, mountains climbed, torrents forded, giants, witches, demons defeated, the fearful guardians of the land of the dead either tricked or cajoled into affording the living hero passage into the forbidden realm. The practice of including weapons and money in the graves of the dead reflects this belief; for of course it is in the steps of the heroes of religious mythology that the dead set out on their journey, and it is in their strength and with their assistance that they hope to arrive at the right destination. In the meantime, however, the going may be expected to be hard enough, and the dead person will need all the assistance he can get, from human as well as divine sources. Thus men co-operate with divinity in provisioning the departed in funeral rites all over the world. These are essentially corporate rites, expressions of the solidarity of the living and the dead. The newly dead have already, during their earthly life, completed a series of difficult and arduous graduation ceremonies which have had the effect of homologising their own life with the heroic career proposed for them by the gods, so that the actions of the survivors in preparing them for this last ordeal are really the culmination of a long process in which men are made progressively more ready for the supernatural identity that awaits them.

Thus the ritual scenario tells us two things about what we may call the authentically religious attitude to death – that attitude of mind which, while taking full account of the circumstances of life in the world which we know, aspires to some kind of transcendence of these circumstances by attaining a superior mode of being. First, it tells us that life is seen as involving a voyage, a journey made up of stages which possess an articulated religious significance. Second, that the voyage is a perilous one; the sufferings, difficulties, hardships and trials that characterise human life are not over for the one who dies until he actually reaches the end of his journey. Indeed, they may even be expected to get worse, and so the living have provided the dead with a symbolic drama of setting forth upon a journey in the company of friends, provisioned and armed by their good offices, encouraged by their goodwill, assisted by their prayers, and with their eventual arrival prepared for them in advance. They have done this so that they may share this symbolic enactment of religious belief with them, and the rite may provide a demonstration or affirmation of the essential solidarity of the dead and the living.[5]

In the typical form of a 'primitive' passage ritual, men symbolise a metaphysical transition by means of an actual geographical progression. They move through a place of chaos into a new territory of enhanced being. This chaotic middle territory is quite literally 'neither one thing nor another':

> The neutral zones are ordinarily deserts, marches and most frequently virgin forests where everyone has full rights to travel and hunt. Because of the pivoting of sacredness the territories on either side of the neutral zone are sacred in relation to whoever is in the zone, but the zone, in turn, is sacred for the inhabitants of the adjacent territories. Whoever passes from one to the other finds himself physically and magico-religiously in a special situation for a certain length of time; he wavers between two worlds. (Van Gennep 1965, p.16)

In the folklore of the world this central territory between life and death, real life and final destination, is the place where ghosts originate, the kind of ghosts who return to haunt the living. They are departed spirits who can get no farther in their journey. They are trapped here and find it easier to return to their old haunts than to continue their journey onwards. They are present-less entities, possessing both

---

5   Cf. Eliade (1954, 1957, 1958a, b). A great deal has been written on this subject, both with regard to initiation rituals and the way that these are expanded into mortuary rites (cf. Habenstein and Lamers (1963) on the Cuna Indians (p.616); Eliade on the funeral rituals of Malekala (1958a, p.62; and Malinowski (1974, p.134)). For the insertion of grave-goods, vide The Funeral Motif of Dismissal, p.52, section e.

history and potentiality, but no *reality*; thus they are the archetypal expression of incompleteness, the very essence of unfinishedness – or they would be if they had an essence. They are inessential entities, useless, purposeless, endlessly wandering. It is their desire for reality which makes them malevolent, and the persistence of their unwelcome attentions is due to an understandable desire to be human again. They come and go as they please, possessing bodies which are ideational only, passing through any obstacle of place or time, because they are subject to no human laws; which indeed is the root of their problem and the reason for their wandering.

A relationship exists between these entities, the supposed inhabitants of the no-man's land between life and death, and the funeral rituals with which all mankind, without any significant exceptions at all, greets the occurrence of the phenomenon of human dying. Looking at this relationship, we hope to throw light on the particular significance of funerals, and the reasons for their social and personal importance. Certainly, the ghosts we shall be considering are our own awareness of those who have not yet been established in being, and who are in their present state a source of anxiety and concern to us. Whether we are dealing only with an *awareness*, and not engaging in the scientific study of objective entities, I do not know. It may be that ghosts exist in themselves, or it may be that they are projections of ourselves, either of particular individuals among us who are able to externalise and objectify an aspect of their own subjectivity; or of a particular relationship between person and person; or of a particular person and the rest of humanity. It has been suggested that the self concerned is able to make use of a source of energy which we have not yet succeeded in properly identifying and measuring. Certainly many selves seem to find the secret; ghosts have been called 'the best authenticated phenomenon in history' (Maple 1964, p.6).

As cultural anthropologists are well aware, concern for the welfare of the dead is very widespread and resists the attempt of reductionists to treat it as the disguised manifestation of something else; and religiously aware scientists have begun more and more to 'take ghosts seriously', examining them as part of the objective universe. Dr Kenneth McAll's (1982) isolation of a 'possession syndrome', which involved the examination of 280 cases of alleged demonic possession and their treatment from a sympathetic point of view – that is, with the willingness to admit the hypothesis that the men, women and children might actually have been 'taken over' by some kind of alien identity inimical to their own – certainly seems more scientific than the attitude of mind which dismisses such matters out of hand. Science, after all, depends on the willingness to test hypotheses. Dr McAll's claim is that the supernatural origin of possession is demonstrated by the fact that it responds to treatment by religious techniques, notably to the rite of exorcism. In many of the cases he records, the specific kind of exorcism employed involves the celebration of a Requiem Mass for the souls of the dead. (I have before me as I write a copy of the particular form of service used by Dr McAll and other members of the Anglican 'Study Group on Christian Exorcism'. It is primarily a service of commendation and an invocation of the Holy Spirit, focused in the sacramental presence of Christ, to 'grant rest' to the departed spirit.) Dr McAll and his associates maintain that in almost all of these 280 cases, the patient's condition has been greatly improved by this approach; and he declares that if it is to retain its dignity as a science, psychology should pay attention to the statistics and not be ruled by 'rationalistic' prejudice.

However, we are mainly concerned here not with ghosts themselves, but with people who believe in them; people who act as though they believe in them; and people who, starting from a position of scepticism, discover in the event that they actually do believe in them. In other words, our investigation is about the 'how' of haunting rather than the 'what' of ghosts. It is also about the significance of funeral rituals and the particular part they seem to play in relieving the distress of the haunted. My own position could perhaps be described as being aware of a religious possibility rather than accepting a scientific fact. Like the majority of people who live in twentieth-century Europe, I resist the idea of the existence of supernatural beings of any kind. But I am conscious of certain psycho-spiritual stirrings when the subject of ghosts is mentioned. I identify this as a religious feeling, not only because I associate divinity with a feeling of awe, but because I believe, quite literally, that there are all manner of things which may be true without my being capable of appreciating their truth. I am quite willing to believe that my scepticism about unwanted 'visitors from another world' has more to do with the limitations of my own perceptual equipment than it has with the objective impossibility of such occurrences; after all, 'with God, all things are possible'. Again, I am perfectly sure that if such things do happen it is for some important human reason, some reason involving the value of persons, which value is great enough to allow a suspension of the ordinary laws of cause and effect. This again suggests to me the presence and involvement of divinity. Ghosts, to me at least, are epiphanous: they demonstrate divine truth as a salutary and purposeful gesture.

Consequently, when I speak and write of them I use the picture language of metaphors. I use the same language that the rite uses, for ritual alone is able to discuss such matters. In *Ghost and Ghoul*, Lethbridge (1967) suggests that exorcism succeeds in 'laying ghosts' because, having once got into the 'wavelength' used by some personalities to transmit a tangible awareness of their presence in their own actual absence, it manages somehow to scramble the message they are seeing by 'interjecting nonsense on the same wavelength' (p.40). He could not, I think, be wider from the mark. The instruction to depart 'in the Name of God' is precisely what the ghost wants and needs to hear. It is the right rejoinder, the clinching argument. He needs to depart 'in the Name of God': in no other way, according to no other Name, *can* he go.

This is the proposition: that ghosts are entities which do not exist but who want or need to exist. That is, they do not exist as *people*. The funeral service establishes them in being, so that they are restored to their previous identity as some kind of person. In religious language this means that the funeral service permits dead people to achieve their religious destiny, whether this is seen as going to a definite place or achieving a definite state of being. Until this has happened, however, they remain trapped in the no-man's land which is envisaged in, and symbolised by, the central portion of the rite.

In mankind's apprehension of his own final destiny – and consequently of the meaning and value of his present existence – the rite is basic. It is the primal mode of religious thought, because it is the most immediate way of expressing a common understanding, an awareness which cannot yet, and perhaps cannot ever, find adequate words. As Professor Gordon Davies has said, 'Ritual would appear to be natural to man ... worship is primary, theology secondary' (1972, p.v). It is not hard to see why, in the religious thinking of so many cultures, the rite is believed to have actual power over life and death. According to E.O. James, it was not belief in ghosts but the creation of rituals to control them that gave rise to the idea of immortality, so that it is the funeral which determines the final condition of the dead (1958, p.118). The rite is used to express existential movement undertaken in testing circumstances. The circumstances are testing because the movement is from a lower, or easier, existential position, to a higher or more difficult one; difficult to attain, that is. It is an essential movement, both from the social point of view and from the religious one, and the mythology with which religious belief naturally and instinctively clothes itself provides the scenario of a radical personal and social change. There is evidence to suggest that the rite of passage is the original corporate religious action, the typical gesture of religious aspirations on the part of a particular culture; and its individual members.[6] In funeral rituals this mechanism is applied to the task of speeding the individual on the last stage of his journey – getting him to heaven, in fact. If it is properly carried out, the suggestion is that it cannot fail.

Among people who subscribe to a system of religious belief this is more than a suggestion. It is an article of faith. It is presented very clearly, as we have seen, in the *Bardo Thodol*, the Tibetan Buddhist textbook about death. It is implied very strongly in both Christianity[7] and Islam. John Layard, writing about the religious beliefs of the people of Malekula in Melanesia, tells us that, 'It is not death but ritual which opens the way to future life. The moment when the ghost sets out

---

6   Cf. Van Gennep (1965) and Turner (1974).
7   Catholic Christianity reserves heaven for the baptised; but only the baptised may receive Christian burial! For the significance of the Requiem, see Evans-Wentz (1960, p.LXXV).

ritual which opens the way to future life. The moment when the ghost sets out upon its way is not the moment when the body dies, but that at which the body is committed to the ground with due observances'(1934, p.118).[8] Some examples of both these aspects of essential funeral behaviour, *committal*, either to the ground, the flames or the elements, and specific *religious ceremonies* undertaken for the repose of the dead, are given below:

- Among the Moslem population of Turkey, the action of burying the dead is considered to be meritorious, so that men and women are eager to take part in the funerals of complete strangers. (A similar attitude is associated also with Judaism and also with the Christian Church, where burial of the dead is listed among the 'acts of corporal mercy' (Habenstein and Lamers 1963, pp.162, 195).)

- According to Westermarck, the Bataks of Sumatra, 'know no greater disgrace than to be deprived of burial' (Bendann 1930, p.49n).

- Among the Burmese Kachins, 'an old and respected chief, if not properly buried, will cause a drought or deluge, destroying the crops of the whole community' (Frazer 1933, p.46).

- Among the Melanesians, 'burial is regarded as a benefit to the ghost; if a man is killed anywhere and his body is not buried his ghost will haunt the region' (Bendann 1930, p.45). The 'curse of Nakaa' was supposed to fall upon the inhabitants of the Gilbert and Ellice Islands so that 'the ghosts of the dead walked in their hearts' if they omitted to bury the bodies of plague victims even though they themselves might be too ill to do so (Polson, Brittain and Marshall 1953, p.9). Similarly, a lost body among the Ikongo of Madagascar 'provokes the relatives of the deceased to make great efforts to discover and return it'. If a drowned body cannot be found, the Ikongo hold a service over the dead person's mat and pillow, which are then buried instead of the remains (Habenstein and Lamus 1963, p.307). Habenstein and Lamers also record that the Ba Venda of the Transvaal are accustomed to holding funerals for those who have died away from home in order to

---

8   Cf. Malinowski (1974). The use of sanctified ground is of the greatest importance and much stress is laid on the ritual confession of reception of the sacrament by the dying – Viaticum, 'food for the Journey'. Actually, the idea of death as a journey and of the effectual intercession of survivors which provides its motive power is fundamental to the Catholic awareness. The prayers and masses which represent the sacrifice of Christ in his natural and mystical body – that is, community of baptised believers – are, in the traditional phrase, 'the wind that fills the ship's sails, as it crosses the perilous ocean of Purgatory'. According to the Council of Florence (1438 – 58), the prayers of the faithful are able to reduce the sufferings of souls in purgatory and ease their entrance into heaven.

'quiet the ghost'; having thus received a grave, it is hoped that the spirit will rest (p.287). The Dakota Indians make the greatest efforts to recover the bodies of those who have died while away from home on a hunting expedition (Habenstein and Lamers 1963, p.689). (Among the Balinese, if the body is not available for cremation an image of the dead person is burned instead!) In the same situation, the Indian Khasis throw seeds into the air at a neighbouring crossroads and carefully gather them up again, 'the seeds representing the bones of the departed' (Bendann 1930, p.47).

- In Samoa burial itself is obligatory, and no other mode of disposal may be substituted for it. The ghosts of warriors slain on the battlefield and thrown into the river return to haunt their survivors, crying out 'oh how cold' (Bendann 1930, p.49n).

- Chinese folk religion credits an individual with two souls. If interment is not correctly carried out, the 'lower' of these, the *kwei* or 'animal soul', is believed to have the power to re-enter the corpse and prey, vampire-fashion, upon the survivors (Habenstein and Lamers 1963, p.1). The Chinese also possess a special rite for summoning back the spirits of those who have died away from home. If at a later date the body is recovered, the usual funeral takes place, and a white cock is carried on the coffin 'to crow for the soul's return to accompany the body'(Habenstein and Lamers 1963, p.25). Confucius held that the immediate disposal of the dead showed the great virtues of submission and love of superiors. Funerals have always been regarded as of the highest significance in China; Marco Polo records that people who believed they had suffered an insult at the hands of an important man would commit suicide on his doorstep so that he would have to provide them with a satisfactory funeral! (Polson *et al.* 1953, p.21.) Habenstein and Lamers record that, 'no more righteous act can be conceived than that of burying stray bones and covering up exposed coffins'. They mention a 'Society of Neglected Bodies', which traditionally has the job of supervising Chinese graveyards (p.27).

'Christian burial' is taken to mean 'the disposal of the dead with appropriate ceremony', and in the same way it is difficult to distinguish, in this world-wide 'compulsion to bury', the actual action of disposal from the rites and ceremonies that inevitably accompany it. For instance, Habenstein and Lamers (1963, pp.230, 231, 266), talking about mortuary rites among the Nigerian Yoruba, the Baganda of Uganda and the natives of Dahomey, simply record that in these places neglect of adequate funeral ceremonies is believed to prevent the dead person from reaching his heavenly destination. However, it is certainly not simply the action of burial alone that decides the fate of the dead, because the same ideas and beliefs are present in cultures where the disposal of the body takes place by other methods. The important thing everywhere would seem to be the *way* that it is done. It must be done with a solemn and formal intention. It is not to be approached in a haphazard or irreverent manner. It is religion we are concerned with, not hygiene. The dead are passed onwards, not simply 'sanitised away'.

- In the absence of the body of the dead person, a Tibetan Lama performs the funeral ritual 'in spirit' (Habenstein and Lamers 1963, p.78). Buddhism is, of course, a highly developed religion, and it is not surprising that the actual presence of the body is not considered essential for the funeral rituals to be properly carried out. The same might be expected to apply in the case of funerals among Christians; or at least among those who adhere to the Catholic belief that religious ceremonies have an essential significance, so that the final commendation of a Christian to God when carried out by his fellow Christians, is a meaningful action and one regarded favourably by God. Many Protestant Christians, however, deny the significance of passage rites of any kind, and see God as being concerned only with the conduct of ordinary 'secular' life. The traditional statement of their attitude to funerals is contained in Ecclesiastes II:3: 'in the place where the tree falleth, there it shall be'. In Laos, ghosts are commonly supposed to wander disconsolately in the nether regions if they are denied parting gifts to pacify them. This is a folk-belief version of the real Buddhist attitude (Habenstein and Lamers 1963, p.98).

- In Vedic India, among those Hindus who pay special attention to the traditional Hindu scriptures, cremation is afforded a sacramental significance. Bendann (1930, p.47) informs us that Hindu children are themselves threatened with death by starvation if they disobey the injunction to carry out the funeral rites of their parents. The *Sraddha* ceremony for the dead is considered essential, for 'verily there are deaths in all the worlds, and were [a man] not to offer oblation to [the gods], death would get hold of him in every world' (*Katapatha Brahmana*). The relatives of Hindus who have died must be immediately informed, so that they can perform this ceremony as quickly as possible, and continue to do so on every succeeding anniversary (Poison *et al.* 1953, p.243). The *Rig Veda* contains a series of rites aimed at allowing the unhoused ghost to enter into the presence of Yama, 'in the abode of light and sparkling waters, clothed in a glorious body enjoying untold bliss under the name of the Fathers' (Bendann 1930, p.169). These rites cover several years: first of all, before the rites begin, the ghost is only a *preta*, an unsettled and unestablished spirit,

able to return to the land of the living. Next, and as a result of the
appropriate ceremonies, it is admitted to the *manes*, becoming their
sapinda, Finally, a year or more later, comes an elaborate rite in which
the bones of the dead man are taken out of the funeral urn and buried
in a suitable place, marked by a monument. The fact that human beings
usually die before reaching the age of 100 used to be explained as a
result of inadequate propitiation of these spirits who concern
themselves with the affairs of the dead, who demand a secret ceremony
which is known only to the initiated (Bendann 1930; Habenstein and
Lamers 1963; Polson *et al.* 1953).

- The same kind of traditions and beliefs abound among the aboriginal
peoples of North America. The dying members of the Salish tribe, for
instance, must confess their sins to a tribal elder appointed to watch
over them to make sure that their departure is a peaceful one. As
Bendann says, 'The principle is invariably the same. The dead would
"walk" unless the body is disposed of with appropriate ceremony'
(1930, p.45). Among the Dakotas (who, like the Chinese and the
ancient Egyptians, believe that a man has a pair of souls), inadequate
ceremony is supposed to cause the 'familiar' soul to haunt the family
and prevent the 'travelling' soul from setting forth on its journey to the
land of the dead: 'whether the deceased Dakota is considered as a lost
loved one, or a fearful ghost, he is at rest only after his kinsfolk have
performed the funeral rites' (Habenstein and Lamers 1963 p.693). In
fact the Santee Sioux of Dakota believed that each man possessed four
souls – but only two of these were affected by the performance of
funeral rituals!) Similarly, the Iroquois hold that the happiness and
well-being of the dead depend upon their funeralisation, and they take
the greatest pains to recover the bodies of their warriors (Bendann
1930, p.47n). The Navaho, on the other hand, 'are concerned solely to
protect the living against death. Stinginess on the part of the living
[that is inadequate provision of grave goods] will bring swift and
terrible retaliation' (Kluckhorn, quoted in Bendann 1930, p.47n). The
Missouri Indians, according to Frazer, are obliged to mourn their dead
with feasts and sacrifices lasting for the remainder of their own
lifetimes at the risk of enduring dream visitations in the form of
'whistling sounds and startling visions' (1933, p.74). The Jivaros of the
Eastern Andes possess an interesting tradition according to which a
dead man's property is shared out among his survivors by playing an
intricate game involving a symbolic canoe, which is used as a die. If
this game is not played, the dead man is expected to be seriously
offended, for he uses it as a means of communicating his wishes to his

kinsfolk (Habenstein and Lamers 1963, p.623). (The parallel with the European ouija board is obvious!)

Many cultures are quite explicit about what they expect to happen if funeral ceremonies are either ignored or inadequately performed, and it is in this context that we discover the most vivid traditions about the activities of ghosts and vampires:

- The Toda believe that it was as a result of neglect of funeral ceremonies that death itself came into the world. When the first Toda died, says Bendann (1930, p.27), some of his brothers and sisters omitted to mourn him properly and, as a consequence, mortality has affected the sons of men ever since.

- The Copper Eskimos hold that the dead are transformed into evil and avenging spirits if the taboos surrounding death and its accompanying rituals are in any way broken (Habenstein and Lamers 1963, p.666). The natives of New Holland fear *ingnas*, 'the spirits of departed men who have been denied funeral rites', *Ekimma* are Syrian vampires who prey upon the living for the same reason (Masters 1974, pp.169, 170), as do *bhatas* in India (and of course *pretas*, whose activities we have already noted above). Among the Indian Kurns, 'even if it is not possible to carry out the funeral rites owing to the absence of the body', the deprived spirit is transformed into a *pesacha* or foul wandering ghost with a strong inclination to take revenge upon the living by many violent acts,' (Bendann 1930, p.7). Frazer notes that the Korkus of Central India expect to be harried by the spirits of the dead until a final ceremony of farewell has been performed, 'several months or even years after the death'. (These spirits have the ability to afflict their living relatives with bodily aches and pains. A similar belief about the power of the dead to cause illness also existed among the Birhors, the Orokaiva of British New Guinea, the Nyanjas of Nyasaland, the Banyankole, the Kenyan Kavirondo and in the Belgian Congo. These examples are all given by Frazer who, as we have seen, was principally concerned with pointing out the ambivalent nature of the relationship which exists between the living and the dead. He mentions those cultures, mainly in Africa, about whom he was best informed. However, it is at least likely that other nations have similar beliefs about the origins of sickness and death (Frazer 1933, pp.49, 144, 147, 151, 157, 162).

- European vampires are well documented. According to the folklore of Catholic countries, they are to be regarded as spirits who have somehow managed to escape from purgatory (Lavater 1572).[9] Ancient tradition among the Serbs of Yugoslavia considers the use of candles at a funeral to be so important that their absence may result in the departed's changing into a vampire and preying on his successors (Habenstein and Lamers 1963, p.482). In Poland, sudden or unnatural death is particularly dreaded because the person concerned is thereby deprived of the opportunity to receive the ministrations of the Church while he is still alive. If he does not make his peace with God, he too is liable to be transformed into a vampire. Great care was formerly taken to make sure that the jaws of corpses were securely tied up so that they would not be able to bite their victims (Habenstein and Lamers 1963, p.446).

These latter examples are of traditions existing within a Christian culture, as are all the stories about Rumanian and Transylvanian vampires. Here again, as with Irish wake cultures the force of primitive belief and custom concerning the desires, needs and intentions of the dead has survived repeated attempts of 'official' Christianity to suppress it. According to Masters, the majority of the stories which abound in Eastern Europe concerning the exploits of bloodsucking ghosts and 'revenants' originate in a terror of people who have died without making confession of their sins, or in a state of excommunication as a result of suicide, or having committed some heinous crime, or simply because circumstances have prevented their receiving the last rites of the Church: 'heading the list of likely candidates for vampirism' (in Greece) 'apart from ex-communicants and those subjected to a curse' are 'those who do not receive the full and due rites of burial' (Masters 1974, p.12). Many vampire tales originate as a result of inadequate burial during times of plague, and Bendann (1930) notes that the Rumanian peasantry considered the impossibility of performing adequate funerals for the dead soldiers and civilians to be one of the principal tragedies of the 1914–18 war (p.50n).

Vampires were well known, it seems, both in ancient Assyria and Babylon, and the connection between funeral rituals and the idea of the dead 'resting in peace' is certainly very ancient indeed. According to the Babylonian *Epic of Gilgamesh*, 'the spirit of him whose body lies unburied will find no rest in the underworld, and it will be forced to eat garbage thrown into the streets'. In ancient Egypt, also, the recovery of the dead body and its proper ritual treatment was considered to be a matter of the very greatest importance, as only ritual embalming was able to

---

9   Cf. Masters (1974) and Gelder (1994). An interesting modern view is put forward by Herschel Prins (1984, p.4).

ensure life beyond the grave. The lore surrounding the funerals of the kings of Egypt provides us with a classic instance of the religious form taken by 'funeral deprivation'. In the ancient texts referring to the royal dead, ritual and life in the next world are treated as one unbroken continuity. Frankfort quotes a sixth dynasty text in the form of a prayer: 'The Venerated who has united himself with the earth, may he traverse Heaven and mount to the Great God' (1948, p.113). The ritual act was considered to operate on two levels. It assured the authority of the departed spirit in the country of the dead, and it also established that of the dead king's successor in the land of the living.[10]

The principle which began with royalty was extended to include commoners also: 'Every Egyptian was similarly dependent on his son for the funerary service which ensured his safe entrance and blessed existence in the Hereafter ... The essential feature of the funerary cult is the absolute dependence of the dead upon those who possess the secret and substance of life (Frankfort 1948, p.208).' Egyptian funerals provided, 'an excellent example of those rites of passage which, with elaborate symbolism, allusions and precautions, guide man's personality from an earlier to a new state of life at each of the crises of birth, puberty, marriage and death' (p.133). Such a rite was especially necessary for the dead, because they of all people, must somehow be moved onward into a new kind of life, and could not simply remain in their present state of non-being. 'The Egyptians like many other peoples conceived of a transitional stage after death, but before the ritual of interment has effected resurrection into the hereafter. In this phase', continues Frankfort, 'man was conceived as neither dead nor alive. It was a period of suspense in which the vital force ... rests' (p.63). The Egyptians knew this 'vital force' as the *Ka* and it was this essential soul or religious identity of each person that was laid to rest by the proper performance of funeral rituals. However, the dead man was also believed to possess a kind of secondary soul, his *Ba*, which took advantage of this intermediary stage of pre-ritual inertia on the part of the *Ka* to 'flit back to its former haunts' among the living. The visits of the *Ba* of a dead man were not to be dreaded, however, as it had none of the vicious or resentful qualities associated with ghosts in other cultures. It was certainly not a vengeful Babylonian vampire – more like a pathetic reminder of the unhappy condition of the *Ka*, as in its intermediate state it longed for rebirth in the land of the sun god.

The Greeks, however, really feared the ghosts of the unburied. During his sojourn in limbo, Odysseus encounters vampire spirits who need human blood to give them the energy to speak. The Greek belief was, of course, that the soul of a

10   'The burial of a king is the same mystery as the coronation empowering his successor'. Cf. the declaration of Neferhotep, a king of the thirteenth dynasty: 'I am in his great office which he gave [to me]. [I am] an excellent son who forms [literally 'begets'] the one who formed [literally 'bore'] him' (Frankfort 1948, p.205).

dead man could not enter the Elysian Fields, the 'abode of blessed spirits', until his body had been buried.[11] The epic literature of the Greeks abounds with references to the taboo surrounding the unburied. The Trojan War itself is held up so that Hector may receive a proper funeral; Agamemnon calls down vengeance upon his wife who, having murdered him, 'would not take the trouble to draw down my eyelids or to close my mouth in death' (*Odyssey*, 15, 66) Hector begs on his knees, not for his life, but that his body might now be thrown unceremoniously to the dogs; King Priam beseeches Achilles to deliver up his son's body for burial; Elpenor's shade pleads that he may receive proper burial, even though his death was the result of his own drunkenness. A third of the *Iliad* is taken up with the attempt to reclaim the bodies of Patrocius and Hector in order to bury them properly. So great in fact was the horror of non-burial among the Greeks that the bodies of dead enemy soldiers were returned to their own armies to receive appropriate passage rites. As with the Chinese, the duty of burying dead strangers was incumbent on all travellers, and passers-by would scatter earth upon the corpses of strangers found by the wayside. Pausanias informs us that it is, a sacred and imperative duty to cover over the dead in this way; Lysander is condemned for failing to bury Philocles and 4000 prisoners.

The Roman attitude to the unburied seems to have been much the same. In the *Aeneid* a great deal is made of the hero's duty to lay to rest the body of King Polydorus, who had been inadequately buried by the King of Thrace, and Palinurus' ghost, like Elpenor's, is ceremonially delivered from the consequences of an unprepared-for death which, in this case, would have necessitated his wandering homeless for 100 years. Aeneas curses the dead Tarquitus with the words, 'Your mother shall never lay you fondly in the earth, or consign your remains to any stately family tomb (Book VI).'

It was commonly believed that the souls of unburied people, being denied access to the nether world, were accustomed to roam disconsolately in the world of men, occupied in the performance of mischievous acts. If for some reason a Roman could not be buried, either because his body could not be found or because it had fallen into the hands of the enemy, his family would set aside an empty tomb and his heir would perform special ceremonies of cleansing and atonement. According to Puckle (1926), the ancients dreaded having no resting place more than the most violent means of death, and in fact denial of burial was used by them as the most terrible punitive sanction of all in dealing with desperate criminals.

---

11   Cf. Tertullian, *De Anima* LVX. Classical literature also has its references to vampires, called *lamiae* by the Greeks and *striges* or *mormos* by the Romans. Both Euripides and Horace mention their exploits. Horace and Ovid accuse them of sucking children's blood.

Apart from the examples already quoted from the epic literature of Greece and Rome, stories about the wandering ghosts of the unburied abound in the works of classical writers. Suetonius records as a historical fact that the body of Caligula was 'disinterred and reburied according to prescribed form' because it had not been disposed of with appropriate ceremony – 'the soul was not at rest, but continued to appear to the living' (Bendann 1930, pp.48, 49n.). Pliny gives examples of other restless spirits satisfactorily dealt with in the same fashion.

To sum up: The belief has existed for thousands of years that the spirits of those whose bodies go unburied wander about the earth seeking rest or intent on mischief of some kind or other. In its primitive form this belief persists in the official religions of some Australian, Melanesian, African and North American peoples; in most highly developed cultures, it inhabits the twilight zone which exists between religion and folklore. It was an article of faith among Aztecs, Chaldeans, Assyrians, Egyptians, Babylonians, Greeks and Romans. Buddhism, Hinduism, Judaism and Christianity all preach the vital importance of adequate funeralisation of the dead, with varying degrees of explicitness about the penalties involved in disobedience, whether this be the miserable half-life of existence in the *preta-loka* of Buddhists and Hindus, or the ghastly dishonour which Isaiah prophesies of those who are not allowed to rest in peace in their graves: 'All the kings of the nations lie honourably, each in his tomb, But you, you have been expelled from your graves Like loathsome dung' (Isaiah 14:18, 19).

Hebrew tradition has it that the gates of *Sheol*, the abode of the dead, are kept securely locked. It would be impossible to record all the stories which have been written about the unwelcome return of the unhappy dead. In addition to the immense amount of imaginative writing on the subject, there is a huge corpus of folklore from which many of the wholly fictional accounts originally sprang. It would not be overstating the case to say that every nation and culture under the sun has its own heritage of ghost tales. They are not, of course, all different. Indeed, in a sense they are all very much the same, for they all tell of unhappy souls who in some way or another have been prevented from achieving their true destiny, stopped from going to their appropriate place. This is only to be expected, however, in the light of the tremendous importance which mankind places on the 'right' treatment of death, whatever may be a particular society's conception of what actually constitutes rightness in such cases. If proper funerals are so important, so *vital*, it would indeed be strange if the souls of men and women who have been deprived of this most basic right of all were not expected by the rest of surviving society to be at least unhappy, and probably extremely resentful as well: hence all the stories, traditional or simply fictional, about the distracted and vengeful dead. When a subject plays such a fundamental part in the shared imaginative life of the human race, the idea of its artistic products being 'simply fiction' may be regarded as something of an over-simplification, and we begin to wonder whether all these stories, passed on from father to son across the ages or 'invented' specially for publication, are not really one version of a single archetypal ghost story, the artistic or formal expression of unconscious knowledge about the promises and perils of immortality which belongs not to individuals but to the human race as a whole.

In the next chapter we shall be trying to arrive at some kind of conclusion as to why the ceremonial disposal of the dead should be so important. For the present, however, we shall remain on the relatively firm ground provided by the evident desire on the part of the living to be properly buried, or cremated, or exposed to the elements – properly disposed of; and equally importantly, that their loved ones should receive the same treatment that they demand for themselves. Sometimes the second desire seems to outweigh the first, and its expression is considerably more striking and perhaps more appealing as well: the picture presented by the British defenders of Maiden Castle as they crept out under cover of darkness to bury those who had fallen victim to the onslaught of Roman invaders commends itself more to modern people than their custom of including in their equipment a cauldron for the purpose of rendering down their own corpse so that their bones could be carried back home for burial. However, this may simply be that concern for others is more attractive than concern for oneself. I remember an elderly Black Country woman telling me that she felt 'much better' when she had visited her sister's grave and made sure that it was neat and freshly adorned with flowers, but as for herself, 'they can chuck me on the rubbish heap if they want!'.

The most celebrated literary example of the compulsion to bury the dead with proper ceremony concerns someone else's body and not one's own. 'My brother's burial I will make, and if for making it I die, 'tis well' (Murray 1941, vv. 71– 73). The act whereby Antigone took it upon herself in defiance of her uncle's explicit ruling to bury the dead body of her brother and in doing so sentenced herself to death, has been regarded from diametrically opposed viewpoints by two playwrights, one ancient and the other modern. Sophocles sees it as a straightforward religious action: that is, one which proceeds from an over-riding desire to act in obedience to a divine imperative. Anouilh, on the other hand, regards it as a superb example of self-assertion, something done entirely for its own sake, what Gide calls an '*acte gratuite*'. The question at issue would seem to be whether Antigone is primarily concerned to defy Creon or to obey God. If the former, then the deed is to be treasured because of its irrationality, the obvious absurdity to the non-religious person of risking death in order to perform a service for someone who no longer exists. Such an action may be seen as a symbol of the very purest defiance. However, there is no doubt at all that the original story refers to, and draws its force from, a quite different attitude of mind about dead people. Antigone's main concern is to perform a religious duty *for the sake of her brother's spirit* and out of love for him, which love is not at odds with the conception of religious truth but in complete accord with it. Her obedience to God will benefit Polynices. Being the right thing to do it will also benefit her; but the principal consideration is the spiritual welfare of a beloved brother.

In a way, though, Anouilh's treatment is more interesting, in that it isolates the compulsive nature of the taboo surrounding the disposal of the dead. The story is about integrity, and both playwrights acknowledge this. Neither is in any doubt that the crux of the drama consists in the value of Antigone's action of personal choice. Anouilh sees that decision as more valuable because it is totally unselfish. Polynices has a right to burial, Antigone a duty to perform the act of burial: and there is an end to it. Antigone must do what has to be done. She needs no other reason than the force of the compulsion to do what is culturally believed to be the right thing. The reasons for burial may be superstitious or trivial or even sentimental, says Anouilh, but Antigone believes that Polynices should be buried – that is the vital thing – and she has the right to her opinion. There is no evidence in Sophocles' play that Creon finds Antigone's behaviour perverse rather than simply disobedient. What we have is a simple confrontation between the authority of the ruler and the authority of 'the powers beyond death who abhor and condemn such impiety.'[12] In Antigone's own words, it is the God of Death himself who 'doth his due rite demand'; and the demand of such a personage far outweighs the ruling of any earthly monarch.

Anouilh's Antigone is significant because it stresses the element of irrationality in the compulsion to bury, while Sophocles' version is important in providing yet another example of a religious attitude that we have reason to believe is universal among the races of mankind. We shall be taking a closer look in the next chapter at this 'element of irrationality' and we shall perhaps see that to call it this is to some extent to miss the point, for it is really the attempt to create rationality out of a situation of chaos and to fashion a kind of order out of the total breakdown of meaning; to make existential sense out of propositional nonsense. For the purposes of this chapter, however, Sophocles' play is of more interest to us because it constitutes the classic statement of mankind's religious obligation to dispose of the dead with appropriate ceremony. The same theme crops up in incidental fashion in other plays – in Euripides' *Trojan Women* for example, and also in Shakespeare's *Henry V.*

In *Hamlet* the circumstances attending death and burial are a major theme of the play. The elder Hamlet was decently interred with all the ceremony befitting a mediaeval Christian monarch. But the way in which he actually died, killed by assassins hired for the job by his brother, prevented him from receiving the last rites of the Church. At the beginning of the play his restless ghost implores his son to avenge his murder, for in his present state he can find no peace:

12   Introduction to Gilbert Murray's translation (see also vv.454ff).

> Cut off even in the blossoms of my sin
> Unhousel'd, unanointed, unannel'd;
> No reckoning made, but sent to my account
> With all my imperfections on my head. (Act I, sc. V)

Like *Macbeth, Hamlet* is a tragedy about the encroaching power of God. Claudius' action in engineering his brother's death is seen as not only wicked in the straightforward sense, indefensibly immoral, but specifically irreligious: iniquitous in the technical, ritual sense, an action of blatant godlessness. When Hamlet himself begins to be subtly corrupted by the forces of evil which have been let loose in the world by this impiety, he acts in exactly the same way and has his former friends, Rosencrantz and Guildenstern 'put to sudden death. No shriving time allowed' (Act V, sc. ii). Sure enough, he finds himself in a situation in which he must act quickly in order to keep himself alive, a situation of simple self-defence, but he is quite specific about the way in which he wishes to defend himself; not only human revenge is sought, but also divine condemnation of his persecutors.[13]

Hamlet is especially interesting to us because it takes two ideas about ghosts and haunting which are frequently found together and holds them in balance so that we may see their real relationship to each other. The ideas are these: that ghosts are the result of inadequate funeralisation, and that ghosts are the spirits of people who have died in tragic or traumatic circumstances; death as a result of crime, committed either against or in some cases by the deceased. Both these ideas are ways of saying that the death in question is fatally or tragically marred; that things are not as they should be because a life has not been properly achieved, and the event of dying is somehow stillborn. As a result, the dead person's life-career has been left in suspense. The religious ritual of the funeral is specifically designed to 'finish things off'; and we can see how such rituals are likely to fulfil a deep psychological need when death comes suddenly, whether from accident or natural causes. The same need is almost unbearably exaggerated when some kind of injustice or viciousness accompanies the circumstances of dying; in other words,

---

13   Religious rituals play an important part in *Hamlet.* Claudius kneels in prayer for the divine blessing which his unrepentant guilt denies him; the religious significance of Ophelia's suicide is ceremonially established by the 'maimed' funeral rites enacted before us. After all, the central character, Hamlet himself, is the very archetype of a man for whom 'the time is out of joint' (Act I, sc.v). Hamlet is no more at peace than is his father. Before either man or ghost can come to terms with himself, certain significant actions, significant for both god and men, must be performed. The whole play is like a funeral ritual, in which through suffering and sacrifice, the past is laid to rest. The scenario involves the temporary triumph of evil, but in the end, and at considerable cost, the crimes of the past are expiated. Many plays follow this general outline, of course (indeed, it may be said to be the basic shape of the tragic play), but *Hamlet* shares with Greek tragedy a consciousness of the *ritual* significance of what is happening on the stage.

when there is an explicit and unmistakeably moral element present and it is felt that some kind of definite crime has been committed, whether this is publicly acknowledged or not.

These are the occasions when religious funeral rites, with the provision they make for reconciling the principal actor in the drama with God and men, are found to be most meaningful. I hope to say more about this later on. For the time being, it is worth pointing out that the typical ghost story begins with a death in circumstances which are traumatic, that is which involve an element of tragic wrongness: a deception, a betrayal, an unjust deprivation, an act of savage violence, the wrong thing happening in the wrong place at the wrong time, an atmosphere of exaggerated dislocation, a dramatically inappropriate happening, a shatteringly discordant note in an otherwise harmonic progression – and ends, if it ends at all and is still not unresolved, with some kind of exorcism. This is the shape of a haunting, although we recognise the experience itself before it achieves such a shape. Indeed, it forces itself upon us in its shapelessness *because of* its shapelessness, as the unfinished beginning of an event which calls for an ending, an achievement. The urge for wholeness, for the satisfaction of unfinished intentions, is so extreme here that it becomes intolerable and appalling – an absence is felt as an obscene presence. The wordless experience is still best expressed in mystical form, in 'the legend of the shade which appears and demands the burial of its bones ... which forms part of mankind's permanent heritage' (Lovecraft 1973, p.19). It does not surprise us that an unfleshed spirit should be concerned about the disposition of its bones, for what more explicit and dramatic symbol could be found for the search for meaning and structure in the face of the total disintegration of death? As far as the biological life of the human body is concerned, everything depends on the framework provided by our skeleton; and the ritual practices of some races bear implicit testimony to the understanding that new life must cling to this same structural element for survival.[14]

There are two principal motifs involved here: that of *disaster and disintegration* (not simply of biological life but of the metaphysical meaning of life, exaggerated and made critical by the circumstances surrounding a particular death) and that of the agonised demand for *restoration and reintegration* (either already answered by appropriate action undertaken by the living or tragically still awaiting its answer). These two ideas provide the basic scenario of the ghost story, the theme that underlies every tradition of a haunting and inspires the writers of ghost stories the world over. The individual ceremonies which make up the total complex of funeral rituals reveal the fact that these ideas also underlie the specifically

---

14   Cf., for example, the burial practices of Tibetan Lamas in Eliade (1958a) and the prehistoric funerals described by Polson *et al.* (1953).

religious attitude to death and dying. As we have already seen, one of the main functions performed by the religious consciousness is that of making sense out of nonsense and bringing order out of chaos, a function which reaches the very peak of its usefulness at the crisis of a death. Without committing ourselves to the proposition that this is what religion is for we must nevertheless acknowledge, and acknowledge with gratitude, that this is what it does. It makes proper provision for death. Even now, in the secular society of the twentieth century in Europe and North America, it is the particular job of religious agencies to proceed with the formal disposal of the dead, and special arrangements have to be made for a non-religious funeral service. Such funerals may be non-religious, but they do not manage to be non-metaphysical in the strict philosophical sense, Indeed, how can they be if their purpose is to import a transcendent meaning into a cripplingly prosaic happening by drawing attention to its poetic implications, its inalienable human significance? Somehow the dead must be meaningfully integrated within a total *Weltanschauung.* The poetry of Wordsworth and the music of Beethoven are also resonant of an overarching meaning, an ideal wholeness, even if they do not transmit the message in the language of St Paul and St John.

There is no doubt that the offices of the Church are of the very greatest use, however. In the days when the only available funeral was an ecclesiastical one, and the services of the clergy for one reason or another (probably concerning the circumstances of the death) were not forthcoming, alternative ways of dealing with the dead had to be found. One way of doing this was to have recourse to an alternative religion. It is a well-established fact that in many places in the world pairs of religions exist side by side, an older more primitive faith persisting alongside a more developed religion which is acknowledged to be the established faith of the particular culture, while the former possesses the distinctive marks of a magical cult; in other words it is used for purposes which are explicitly forbidden by the 'official' religion. The most obvious example of this is the practice of witchcraft, which has flourished for centuries alongside the Christian institutions of Western Europe. This 'secondary' religion usually claims to be older in origin than its more respectable rival, and offers its devotees the opportunity to learn secrets 'which have remained hidden from the beginning of time,' laying claim to a store of recondite knowledge which remains beyond the reach of younger and therefore less venerable religions. This knowledge will most likely have more to do with the basic concerns of earthly survival than with rules concerning moral behaviour in this dispensation or the final meaning of existence itself.

Such secondary religions, as Eliade (1958b) points out, are often variations on the worship of some kind of fertility goddess or 'earth-mother'; the implication being that the official religion of society, that structure of belief which gives its sanction to social norms and governs the organisation of social institutions, draws its authority from a divinity who cannot be expected to concern himself with basic matters of procreation or with the technical details of life and death on the biological level. He is the god of masculine concerns, of social aspiration and personal holiness, and His mind is 'set on higher things'. Eliade points out that many religions which possess extensive fertility cults hold a well-defined doctrine concerning the existence of a heavenly father-figure, and in such cases, burial rites are likely to be the concern of the secondary and more 'maternal' deity: 'earth to earth, ashes to ashes'. In *The Ritual Process*, W.V. Turner (1974) draws attention to some of the practical purposes to which such a system can be put in preserving the balance of society, both by providing a way of achieving a measure of social conformity for people who wish to opt out of the established structures or are for some reason or anther debarred from membership of them (and here the European equivalent would probably be the Freemasons or Grand Order of Buffaloes rather than with witchcraft, which is still regarded with disfavour by society as a whole), and by allowing a measure of what might be called institutionalised protest. This is negative feeling of a personal or social kind which receives official tolerance, or even approval, being 'taken into the system' and used by society to achieve an internal balance, an overall comprehensiveness, in which dissident elements are comprehended rather than simply excluded (and here, of course, witchcraft might be included). The advantage of such a system with regard to religion is perhaps seen at its best from a psychological point of view, because it permits proper expression of the feminine archetype in the religious consciousness of mankind which, according to Jung at least, is an essential counterpart of the masculine aspect of god-head within the collective unconscious. This is the Anima, which complements the Animus and so forms an integrated whole within the psychic life of the individual and the race. (The most obvious example of this in our own common experience is the veneration paid to Our Lady in the Roman Catholic Church.)

When the dominant religion of a society forbids any ritual form of communication with the spirits of the departed, recourse may be had to less official methods. In Ireland, for example, the ancient pre-Christian religion of the *sidhe*, the aboriginal fairy inhabitants of the land, is traditionally believed to afford the living a way of making illicit contact while avoiding ecclesiastical censure. Many legends tell how the bereaved are accosted by fairy folk who lead them into the presence of the departed. This takes place usually on November Eve at the great Celtic feast of *Samain*[15] when the two races, *sidhe* and ghosts, join in festivals. Such contact runs counter to divine ordinance; the living are warned not to mention the name of God or to cross themselves, for if they do the ghosts will

---

15   The word '*Samain*' is derived from *sam*, 'one' or 'together', and suggests a time when, 'the barrier between this world and the Otherworld was removed and contact with the Gods was close.' (Myles Dillon quoted in Raftery (1964, p.66)).

immediately disappear, by invocation of the laws imposed by a superior religion. Christianity demands that the dead keep their own place and refrain from revisiting the realm of living human beings.[15]

The *sidhe*, perhaps because of the freedom with which they move between the land of the dead and the everyday world of human beings, are very much concerned with the welfare of the departed, and take it upon themselves to make sure that they are treated with the respect and consideration which are their due. One way in which they are traditionally supposed to do this is by taking upon themselves responsibility for caring for the bodies of men and women who, either from ecclesiastical policy or ordinary neglect, have not received proper burial. In this way they make up for any lack of charity on the part of organised religion and normal human society towards the departed.[16]

In this way also they serve to defend society against the very real threat of reprisals on the part of the dead themselves. 'Like children who have not been baptised, named or initiated, persons for whom funeral rites are not performed are condemned to a pitiable existence since they are never able to enter the world of the dead or to become incorporated in the society established there ... These are

---

15   Cf. Lady Wilde (1988). Lady Wilde also refers to legends concerning young girls who have been illegitimately reunited with their dead lovers through the agency of the *sidhe*, and are consequently debarred from attending Mass. The *sidhe* are supposed to be fallen angels, doomed to live among men in perpetual unscathed youthfulness until Judgment Day (was Dorian Gray such a being?), when all the natural human ills they have avoided in their state of protected innocence will be visited upon them. In the meantime they move between two worlds, the world of the living and that of the dead, in accordance with the laws of an ancient pre-Christian religious notion of the relationship between the dead and the living.

16   A folk tale which admirably illustrates this particular point was told to me twenty years ago in County Mayo. It concerns Tim O'Kane, a notorious ne'er-do-well who was turned out of his father's house because of his selfish refusal to marry his sweetheart, whom he had made pregnant. As Tim wandered about the surrounding countryside in the middle of the night, he was accosted by a burial party of the *sidhe*. Tim was paralysed with fear and couldn't say a word when one of the little men came up to him and said 'Isn't it lucky we met you tonight, Tim O'Kane?' he repeated this twice, but Tim's tongue felt as if it was stuck to the roof of his mouth. The little man turned to his companions and said: 'Well, seeing as how Tim hasn't got a word to say we can do with him as we please.' Looking at Tim he said, 'Tim, my boy, you're living a bad life and we can make a slave of you now, and you can't stop us, so there is no need to try. Lift that corpse.' And so the unfortunate young man is forced by his fairy captors to tramp over the whole countryside trying to find a suitable burying place for the burden on his back. He is given a list of places where the body may be buried, but he cannot count on having success in any of them for as the leader of the *sidhe* tells him, 'Maybe the body won't be allowed to be buried ... someone else might be in the grave and wouldn't want to share it with anyone; if you can't bury it in Teampullshemus [that is St James's church] you must carry it to Carrick-a-Durus and try the churchyard there, and if it still isn't possible, take it on to Teampul-Ronan; and if you still cannot bury it, well if you go from there to Kill-Breeda you can bury the corpse without hindrance.' This, in fact, is what happens. At each of the first three places there is some reason why the dead man must not be buried there, and Tim is forced to stagger on, the corpse on his back giving him directions all the while. Advised by

incorporated into the world of the living, and since they cannot be, they behave like hostile strangers towards it' (1965, p.160).

And so vampires are given a second burial to put an end to their gate-crashing activities. This is burial as simple repression, the denial of an unpleasant awareness, an unwanted presence. But in a very real sense the intrusive presence of the undead is connected with the fear of unfinished business, when the business in question is felt to be of crucial importance both to the haunted person and to the person who does the haunting. The truth of the matter is that something has gone wrong. Either the dead person did not want to go, having something vitally important to do before he departed, or the ones he left were unwilling to let him go, unwilling to register his going in the 'right' way and thus ratify it as an event, something giving form to his actual historic lifetime.

As we shall see in the following chapters, to neglect to allow death the significance of a completed process is to refuse to accept it as a happening at all. In the language of religious understanding, this is to give the dead person nowhere to go. Nowhere to go and nothing to do. Ghosts are people who are in the wrong place. People who are 'neither here nor there'. (I am reminded of Fr Herbert McCabe's contention that hell is populated by the souls of people who are unable to die: 'confronted by God but unable to die into him' (1964, p.213)). The funeral is the means whereby they are kept in the right place, in their proper dimension of being. This need not in actual fact be very far away from the living. At least, not in one sense, the sense of relationship and communication, which depends in any case upon a certain amount of real distance. The world of the incorporated and established dead may be understood as impinging upon the world of the living, in some cases even overlapping that world. For purposes of social and psychological integration, many cultures welcome home the very ghosts whom they have been at such pains to send away. By dismissing them formally, giving due acknowledgement to their change of status, they can now accord them proper social recognition. Indeed, the presence of the dead becomes an essential part of the corporate life of society. 'Ghost cultures' incorporate the search for new life, the need for continuity and wholeness of experience by using the past to reinforce

---

the corpse, he tries a fourth burial ground and is turned away from there as well. Finally, at Kill-Breeda he is successful. Tim looks down into the newly-dug grave: at the bottom is a large black coffin. He jumps down and bravely removes the coffin lid, and to his relief, finds it empty ... the corpse which has been holding onto him for over eight hours suddenly relaxes his grip and drops down straight into the coffin. Tim sinks to his knees and prays to God for deliverance. The story is hilariously funny. But it has a serious purpose nevertheless. From that day on, according to tradition, Tim O'Kane was a 'changed man'. With the aid of the *sidhe* he had atoned for his past misdeeds with an act of corporal mercy. He married his girl, whom he had loved all the time but had been prevented from marrying by his wicked way of life. Now at the cost of considerable personal suffering in the way of mental terror and physical hardship, he had succeeded in burying the dead.

the present. A dead person is encouraged by the corroboration of his social and personal identity even beyond the grave to emerge publicly as a 'recognised' ghost, a being with whom the living may have an ongoing relationship.

These officially ratified spirits are not simply wraiths and phantoms, a kind of ex-people who have lost their way on their journey, straying somehow from the path between worlds. They possess power by virtue of being dead. This is their taboo-holiness, which distinguishes them in a positive way from the living. Their ritual otherness, which renders them objects of awe and fascination, allows the living to differentiate them as real beings, active and personal presences, and so enter into genuine relationship with them. The degree of terror that the dead are able to inspire in the living is the measure of the reality of this relationship. They have departed into the realm of the holy, a sphere of being which is privileged precisely because it is so different, so apart, so radically other. The rite has unequivocally *located* them, and now protects us from them by laying down the terms of our interaction with them. It is the awareness of the special holiness of the dead which underlies the preoccupation with ghosts characterising some markedly religious cultures, where the aim is to undergird the structure of society by forming a significant relationship with the ghost-kingdom, whose denizens possess an authority denied to the living, but still available to them through ties of friendship and love which may be kept up across the frontier of the grave.[18]

Thus the realm of ghosts stands in a very special relationship to the world of the living, and a certain amount of interaction is often encouraged to take place between the two spheres. This kind of socially recognised interaction is always rather one-sided, however. It is the living who take the initiative and not the dead. The world of the dead must on no account be allowed to *intrude* upon the world of

---

18   R.E. Bradbury's description of ghost-lore among the Edo shows how central are ideas of authority and status to the particular role played by ghosts in a primitive society, in which the dead and living are conceived of as living in close partnership. 'A primary division must first be made between what I may call the unincorporated dead (ghosts of several varieties) and those ghosts who have been assigned a 'constitutional' position vis à vis the living by a deliberate act of re-incorporation ... In general it may be assured that while relations between the living and the incorporated dead have a strong, positive, moral component, ghosts are dealt with almost entirely in terms of expediency. The incorporated dead are accepted as acting justly in their demands upon the living who are morally obliged to submit to their authority and to sustain them; they are also believed to be capable of conferring positive benefits in the form of vitality and prosperity on their worshippers' (1966, p.131). But it is only the incorporated dead, who have been welcomed back into union with the society they have left *as a result of having left it in the prescribed manner*, who are regarded as friendly and dependable: 'The unincorporated dead act out of anger and resentment untempered with any capacity for exercising benevolence', for they, 'have just grievance against the living ... their heirs have neglected to perform the rites that would convert them into ancestors and elders in the land of the dead' (1966, p.131) Vide the end of this chapter, The Funeral Motif of Chaos.

the living. If it does so, then it may be assumed that something has gone radically wrong at the point of intersection between living and dying.

The funeral rite, the rite of final passage, constitutes this gateway between worlds. In the extended rite, the first movement opens up the way into death and the final one closes it up again. Only in the rite's central space does the door stand open and the two worlds mingle in timeless confusion and fruitful chaos. Even our exiguous modern Western funerals possess this crucial liminal quality, simply by being rituals, symbols of essential change and transformation, acted statements of the truth about an existential landmark, a frontier of life that has been reached and is being crossed. Even in our 'one-movement' funerals we are talking the language of myth. By the action of coming together to accompany a dead man or woman on the first stage of his or her last journey, we use the pictorial language that men have used from time immemorial to embody their very deepest concerns. It is important for us to understand that these ideas – ghosts and vampires, life and death which are objectified as separate territories, with a gateway which stands between them in its own special inbetween place, occupying a pause between time and eternity – correspond to identifiable reactions within the psychological economy of individuals and societies. The trauma of bereavement leaves behind it a chain reaction which finds a special meaning, an uncanny appropriateness, in notions like these. Our minds are invaded by an awareness of the living presence of someone whom we know is dead. It is a disturbing awareness, an unwelcome presence. The knowledge that such haunting is irrational makes us the more determined to ignore it, deny it, repress it; it becomes a complex and produces symptoms of a neurotic kind. We strive to dissociate ourselves from it, and immediately it becomes stronger and more definite. 'This is nothing to do with me,' we say. 'I do not want it. I disclaim responsibility for it. Let it leave me alone. It has no business here. It is a ghost.' And so it is. Somehow the gate between the two worlds has been left open.

The Funeral Motif of Chaos (The Liminal Phase)

1. *Descent into hell*

    a. *Return to the beginning.* When life is overtaken by death, cosmos gives way to chaos; a return is made to the timeless moment that precedes time, and serves as available evidence about God and eternity. 'This theme of going back in order to abolish the historical duration that has already elapsed and to begin a new life with all its possibilities intact, has so obsessed humanity that we find it in a great many contexts and even in highly developed soteriologies and mysticisms.' (Eliade 1958a, p.55). Christian theology, for example, draws attention to the coinherence of beginning and ending: 'The relation between seed time and harvest is one of both identity and difference.' (Williams 1972, p.18.)

b. *The central power house of creation.* Opposites are held in relation by the presence of the divine action which, by separating them, holds them in creative tension. The rite's liminal phase acts as the central clearing-house of forms in which being is dispersed and redistributed prior to reformulation. Here, life is reduced to vagueness and indeterminacy, to harsh discords and violent conflict, the raw material of meaning without any meaning – anarchic, dissonant, confused, self-contradictory. The liminal phase exists to define the existences which contain it; aimlessness and impossibility are welded together by the action of the complete rite into an unambiguous communication about purpose and change, as reality is reconstructed by homologisation with perfection. The rite as a whole symbolises the creative power of God to bring order out of confusion and to make this power available to men and women; its central movement may be characterised as the confusion of existence in the presence of being. The reversal of natural order and the shattering of all ordinary expectation signals the necessary presence of chaos before it can resolve itself into a new universe of meaningful relationships.

c. *Liminal holiness.* This central part of the rite is always forbidden territory, as the ritual scenario itself ensures that it will be as exclusive of the ordinary world as possible, closed off to all not directly involved. The source of this exclusiveness is the presence of death itself, whether we imagine this as a still centre, the heart of a furnace or confrontation with the radically other. Death gives rise to the liminal terror which anthropologists tell us attaches to all frontiers (Douglas 1966, p.121), geographical and territorial as well as existential and personal. Every frontier, each landmark in life, becomes an image of the 'great divide', the ultimate frontier between life and death, and thus the object of a special kind of awe. Thus, radically abnormal occurrences are felt to be holy; wherever we are confronted with the shock of otherness, something for which we are totally unprepared, we are irresistibly reminded of holiness. The presence of the anarchic and irregular in funeral behaviour may be seen as a straightforward reaction to the irruption into human affairs of what Otto (1950) originally called 'the numinous' – the inevitable human reaction to the holiness of God. Death is envisaged as a violent implosion of holiness: violent because of the quality of the event, holy because it forces us to abandon our existing intellectual, emotional and moral organisation and cry out in anguish to a higher source of unity.

d. *The pivotal corpse.* Taboo belongs to everything connected with the dead person, because of the symbolic power attaching to the corpse itself. It is around the ambivalence of the corpse's symbolism that the ritual scenario arranges itself. This more than anything is the reason for the chaos at the rite's centre. In the presence of the corpse the living are pulled this way and that, attracted by what they know, love and understand, repelled by its sudden uselessness and irrelevance. There is no life in the corpse; it is an object of particular horror; there is no life apart from the corpse, for it is like us, it *is* us. The corpse has entered the realm of the sacred; it is this that draws us on and this that repels us. This is the symbolism of the cave-burial, in which the cave is at one and the same time the tomb towards which we travel and the womb from which we emerge. It survives wherever burial is the custom; but even cremation allows the ashes of the dead to be retained in jars, urns and other rounded receptacles. The purpose of symbolism is always to point in two opposite directions at once. The corpse provides a splendid vehicle for this kind of spiritual journey.

e. *The need for purification.* Such a potent symbol must be highly contagious. Ways of avoiding contagion include:

  i. Washing, after contact: ancient Greece, Rome, Persia and so on. (many other cultures throughout the world).

  ii. Avoiding widows and people who have been in close contact with the corpse: Hottentots, Jivaro Indians, Brazilian Kaingang, Guatemala, Zoroastrians, New Caledonia, British Columbia (Shuswap), Thompson River Indians.

  iii. Dealing with the corpse regarded as a special social status: New Zealand (Maori). The Welsh sin-eater belonged to this category. As well as speeding the dead, she or he participated in the taboo surrounding contact with them.

  iv. Restrictions or prohibitions on clothing, food, drink, sexual intercourse, work or entertainment imposed on mourners: Hungary, Africa (Buganda), Hindu (Kumbi, Lohor), New Guinea (Massim, Monumbo), Trobriand Islands, Australia (Gariauna, Geelvink Bay natives, Koita, Tubetube). As Douglas (1966) has pointed out, foods are avoided according to the religious logic of particular cultures. The main reason, however, is their association with the taboo surrounding death. They are not bad foods in the sense of being unhealthy or corrupt; they are simply *special* – temporarily set aside for death.

v. Procedures involving mourners' bodies: faces painted or blackened: Australia (Ngonlango, Hood Peninsula, Duke of York Island): self-mutilation: Melanesia, Indonesia, N. American Indians (Dakota, Jivano).

2. *Reversals of practice as a contribution to chaos*

These are more than changes of direction aimed at confusing the departing ghost; they represent a state of affairs in which nothing is normal any more.

a. *Clothing reversal*: Ethiopian Christian, Japanese Ainu.

b. *Hair either cut short or grown long* (the opposite of normal custom): Ancient Greece and Rome, Ethiopian Christians, Orthodox Jews, Bulgaria, Greece, Malta, S. Italy, Africa (Congo, Gold Coast, Bugandan Edo and Yoruba peoples), Paraguay, Tonga, India (Hindu), Australia (Narrinyeri, Warramunga), American Indians (Arapaho).

c. *Not mentioning the dead person's name*: Australia and Melanesia, S.E. Asia, Panama (Cuna).

d. *Not allowing normal emotion to be shown*: Turkey, Europe (Protestant).

3. *The wake*

a. *Wake traditions inside Europe*: Ireland, England, Scotland, Wales, the Isle of Man; Sweden, Norway, France, Germany, Silesia, Hungary, the Balkans, Rumania, Poland, Estonia (in Germany, Silesia and Hungary, these involved playing games with the corpse itself).

b. *Outside Europe*: North American Indians, Pacific Islands, Ecuador, Brazil, Guatemala (Indian), Mexico, Laos, Ghana (Ashanti), Fanti, Dahomey, Azande, S. Bantu, Madagascar (Menabe, Ikongo), Malabar (Nayars), Bali, Papua, China, Mongolia, Japan.

4. *The ritualisation of grief as a contribution to social confusion*

a. *Salaried mourners*: Ireland, ancient Rome, Lebanon, Ethiopia, Hungary, Ecuador, China.

b. *Ritualised sorrow and anguish*: Poland, Yugoslavia, Ethiopia (Coptic), Philippines, Australia, Melanesia, Fiji, Turkey.

c. *Self-mutilation*: Melanesia, Indonesia, North American Indians (Dakota, Jivaro).

4

The Shape of Death

The unburied soul sent on its way with a Requiem. The cairn of stones to dissuade the restless spirit of a prehistoric nomad from following after his wandering kin-folk. The stake through the heart which imprisons the vampire within his coffin. Symbols of the need to define, to establish a fixed point in a chaotic reality. We have been looking at the universal disposition towards ceremonial disposal of the dead from the point of view of religious obligation. Now we must attempt to approach the subject from another point of view. As we have already said, not all burial is a religious burial, although the act of disposing of the body is almost always accompanied by what we might call a ceremonial invocation of *value*. But why should the body of a dead person require solemn obsequies, unless such obsequies are expressly demanded by religion? And why does religion require them? If we can answer the first question, we may well be able to answer the second one too.

We have already noted that Anouilh's version of the story of Antigone's determination to bury her brother's body differs significantly from the play written by Sophocles (1951). According to the French playwright, the issue is not primarily a religious one; or rather it is not out of respect for the normative rules of religious behaviour that Antigone is risking her own death and the anger of her uncle, Creon. She does not contradict him when he expresses his contempt for the insincerity which accompanies funerals and the superstitious attitude which holds that the dead are condemned to go on wandering about forever for the lack of a bit of earth thrown on the corpse according to a clerical formula:

CREON: And did you never think to yourself that if it was a being whom you really loved lying down there in that box, you would scream out all of a sudden, scream at them to shut up and go away?

ANTIGONE: Yes, I have thought of that.

CREON: And now you want to die because I have refused your brother this derisory passport, this mass-produced mumbo-

> jumbo, this pantomime you would have been the first to be ashamed and sickened by if it had been performed. It's absurd!

ANTIGONE: Yes, it's absurd.

Creon accuses her of disobeying him through pride, '*l'orgueil d'Oedipe*' (1954, p.72, my own translation). But pride is not the reason for her stubbornness any more than is religion. The truth is that Antigone acts in this way because the situation in which she finds herself demands some kind of gesture. To bury Polynices is the most meaningful gesture she can make. It is not, in her opinion, the ideal thing to do. She does not know what that would be. But the circumstances of her action, and the consequences which it bears in its train, give it a certain stature which it would not otherwise possess. They make it more absurd and consequently more important. She acts for the sake of action: and the necessity of having to defend her action with her life gives it a kind of tough personal validity. It is her action, made inalienably her own by the fact that it could commend itself to no one else. Indeed, it could not commend itself even to her on any other terms. Because it is so painful, because of the purity of its painfulness, the absence of compromising circumstances – secondary advantages, overtones of noble self-sacrifice or martyrdom for the sake of religious truths courageously defended, or any other kind of emotional or spiritual perquisite – it is immeasurably important, startlingly significant.

From Anouilh's point of view, this significance comes from the degree of freedom which such an action possesses. Antigone is able to demonstrate the individual as one who is not led by the existence of conflicting interests into the position of compromise which is characteristic of most people's attitudes and actions during most of their lives – and is typified here by Creon, the authoritarian figure who is nevertheless driven continually to act against his better nature, and to give in to outside pressures, to the extent of putting in jeopardy the very things he is striving to protect.

(Antigone: 'You didn't really want to leave my brother's body unburied, did you … yet you did it just the same. And now you are going to have me killed without wanting to. And that's what being a king is!' Creon: 'Yes, that's it!' (p.76))

The crux of the play is located here in the conflict between sensible compromise and foolhardy steadfastness, between the 'adult' man of the world, whose shop-soiled subtleties are a desperate attempt to avoid a greater and more obvious evil, and the inflexible young idealist, whose altruism seems to be inherently self-destructive.

Not intentionally self-destructive, however. It is only the harsh facts of political life and the clash of personal interests that make it so. For Antigone is not trying to kill herself, but to preserve herself; to preserve her self-hood in the face of the disintegrative forces which surround her, the moral degradation of an administration which is willing to resort to a crime against inalienable human dignity, simply to preserve order; to preserve it, too, in the face of the intellectual and emotional impact of personal bereavement, the terrifying synchronicity of cataclysmic happenings which leaves is mark on an entire personal universe. Viewed in this light, her '*acte gratuite*' is a desperate clutching after sanity rather than a suicidal gesture: and it is as such that we are concerned with it here.

In this chapter we shall be examining the funeral as a way of establishing meaning rather than a way of behaving in accordance with a previously understood and accepted meaning: the funeral as an existential gesture rather than as an expression of religious belief. The urge to bury dead people is often given a religious rationale. However, there seems to be some reason to think that this may be a case of 'explanation after the event', and that the impulse is at least pre-doctrinal, if not pre-religious. It is here that the position taken by existentialist writers such as Camus or Sartre is of particular value. This may be summarised as the assertion that, in a life which, in the absence of metaphysical meaning and religious significance, is basically absurd, death appears as the true source of meaning. The final statement gives meaning to the whole essay. Where the period is placed makes sense of the sentence. Man being free from social and religious determinisms – free in himself, in his inner being, or at least able to assert such freedom by a self-determined gesture of soul – is able to decide how that final statement shall be made, and whether the making of it will express courage or cowardice, humility or pride, honesty or deceit; and by doing so he is able to alter the tone of all his previous living, and determine the retrospective value of all his previous actions. This is the artistic view of life, in which a life-career resembles a musical theme, whose impact on the listener is determined by its final cadence. When we realise that the circumstances of human life rarely allow us this much control over the manner of our dying, we have to include the nature of this eschatological final statement in our daily living, our moment-to-moment existence. We cannot leave it to the end, because we have no control over so many things that might happen to us, so many accidents that might befall us. But what we can control, we will. We will make the manner of our going the 'realised eschatology' of our living.

This, of course, is exactly the state of mind urged upon us by religion. We are recommended to live in a state of 'recollection of our own mortality', so that we may be 'ready to give an account of ourselves at the Day of Judgement', or to 'pass through the illusion of appearances with our spiritual gaze fixed upon the promise of enlightenment to come'. Wherever we are, whatever we are, we must retain the very clearest reference to something or somewhere else, and it is this religious reference which gives value to the here and now, making sense of all the contradictory experiences of life, harmonising its discords, synthesising its disparate elements. The testimony of these 'nonreligious' writers, Antigone's testimony, is that this order is self-authenticating and that meaning is necessary for its own sake. Value and meaning and the vision of order are basically necessary for human well-being.

Obviously, we are not really saying very much here; and we are certainly not saying anything which is in any way original. There can be no philosophy of any kind, religious or otherwise, which is unwilling to allow human existence at least the possibility of meaning. The presence of *shape*, either apparent or discoverable, is the presupposition of any conclusion drawn about existence. That is what 'drawing a conclusion' means! But the relationship between the shape of things and their value is worth considering, all the same. Some writers have identified the two ideas and said quite clearly and uncompromisingly that, for human beings the value of events consists in their shapeliness, or in the ease with which the mind can impose a kind of shape upon them and draw conclusions from them. This is done by fitting them into a kind of overall and comprehensive order which the critical intellect finds satisfactory because it is consistent, balanced, whole. Thus religion, as ideal value, is the promise and the presence of ideal shape, of a quality of experience in which the self can rest because it is able to explain and relate everything that happens or could conceivably happen.[1] It follows from this that religion's main purpose is in dealing with death, the shapeless event *par excellence*, the piece of existential jigsaw which always refuses to fit. By postulating an ideal shape which is an infinite extension of human patterns, and an ideal value which is the infinite enlargement of the human facility to create patterns, every kind of unassimilable experience can be accommodated. Religion's capacity to homogenise experience is so wide that the most unpalatable fact of all, the fact of death, may be swallowed whole. Indeed, it must be swallowed whole or it cannot be dealt with at all. It must be part of God's plan, because it so obviously is no part of our own.

As we saw in Chapter 1, this was the idea of the function of religion which occurred to Malinowski when he saw the effect of religious funerary rituals upon bereaved individuals and families among the Trobriand Islanders. We might call it the medical notion of the religious function, because it regards religion as a kind

---

1   'Religion is the audacious attempt to conceive of the entire universe as being humanly significant ... the sacred cosmos emerges out of chaos, and continues to confront the latter as its terrible contrary' Berger (1973, p.37). This idea is also treated by Clifford Geertz: 'There are at least three points where chaos – a limit of events which lack not just interpretations *but interpretability* – threatens to break in upon man: at the limits of his analytic capacities, at the limits of his powers of endurance, and at the limits of his moral insight. Bafflement, suffering and a sense of moral paradox are all, if they become intense enough or are sustained enough, radical challenges to the proposition that life is comprehensible ... challenges with which any religion, however "primitive", which hopes to persist must attempt somehow to cope' (1966, p.14)

of specific for acute existential indigestion. Desperate conditions require desperate remedies. In this case a whole new view of existence must be called into play because at the moment of crisis the old way of reacting to the world of experience has turned out to be totally inadequate for dealing with the situation. The data associated with dying have proved unprocessable by the conceptual computer which handles the code of life's experiences; the shock has blown the system. Another epistemological universe, another kind of knowing, must now be brought in to replace the old one. It is for this emergency that religion is kept officially 'in the picture', and it is at times like this that religious institutions come into their own and justify their place in society.

Whatever we may think of this as an account of the genesis of religion, it must be accepted that, in certain circumstances, the *need* to see the world in a certain way does produce the *ability* to do so. Berger's claim that, 'men are congenitally compelled to impose a meaningful order upon reality' (1973, p.31) is supported by the results of a good deal of psychological investigation. The tendency of the mind to produce constructs is basic to its function. Experience, gained in contact and immediacy, in the lived moment, is always abstracted from the situation to be considered at a distance. This, it seems, is the way we are. Our percepts are inevitably organised into evidence: to use Martin Buber's phrase, we withdraw from 'I–Thou' into 'I–It', so that we may draw conclusions by a process of comparing and relating our findings (1966). We cannot avoid doing this and remain human.

But the process is not confined to human beings. During World War I Kohler's experiments with chimpanzees (1925) threw light on the function of the mind in perceiving reality in the forms of patterns of experience rather than of separate percepts which are painfully assembled, piece by piece. Reality, it seems, was not wholly learnt, it was partly guessed owing to the ability of consciousness to postulate organic connections between the disparate objects of perception. Later investigators have gone further in establishing the existence of an innate tendency towards the meaningful organisation of experience. Ittelson and Kilpatrick (1964), for example, argue that this particular disposition is so strong that it may actually distort our idea of outside reality. We perceive contextually, as Kohler demonstrated, but our experience of familiar contexts, habitual assumptions about reality, leads us into mistakes when these contexts contain unfamiliar data, when reality is in fact very slightly different from what it usually is and what we have come to expect it to be. In other words, there is a tendency for us not to register objects and situations as they are but to draw instantaneous conclusions about them from what we have previously learnt about objects and situations which we presume to have been identical with them. Sometimes, however, our presumption turns out to be wrong. This predisposition towards hanging new experiences on an established mental framework or experience and expectation may lead to the creation of definite 'mental sets' which stand in the way of our arriving at correct solutions to perceptual problems.

In short then, the impulse to 'think contextually' is so powerful that it may cause animals and people to 'see' things that are not there and to overlook things that are. As Festinger(1957) has demonstrated, this is an impulse and not simply a habit. There is a definite tendency towards the organisation of experience into forms which the mind finds satisfying. Indeed, the impulse is so powerful that, in order to achieve the satisfying shaping of experience, perceptual evidence is falsified, tailored to fit an interior design which is the shape of desire rather than the unshapely facts of reality as others see it.[2]

The idea that the mind is able to establish its own meanings and that these will be affected by either habit or positive inclinations, proceeds from the claim made by the psychologists of the *gestalt* school that the brain perceives reality in the form of articulated pictures which possess and impose their own innate consistency. It might be used to provide a 'scientific' explanation for such 'psychic phenomena' as 'place memory', the perceived presence of dead people in places with which in life they had strong associations, and which provided the settings for episodes in which they were involved – episodes so violently traumatic that the place itself invariably calls to mind the incidents that took place in it (although we should still have to account for the tendency on the part of ghosts to appear to people who are entirely ignorant of any such association). In the light of the last chapter, we might experiment with the notion that ghosts are percepts that, having once left their own accustomed *gestalt* (the place where a dead person has lived and worked, the people he has known), are not able to achieve the appropriate new one (the particular picture of the after-death world entertained by a culture or religion), because the original *gestalt* was never properly established or completed, owing to the circumstances surrounding death. Shape in living and dying is both the image of, and the qualification for, participation in the ideal shape of eternity.

However, our main purpose in drawing attention to this here is to provide definite evidence of the existence of an urge towards the assertion of meaning in the face of perceptual disorder. We have been looking at the state of overwhelming existential chaos produced in individuals and groups of people by the happening of death. The death of someone we love has an almost totally disruptive effect on our attempts to make sense of the world we live in. Our personal self-image, the picture we have in our minds of ourselves, is an inclusive one and arranges itself around one or two key relationships, people who stand out

2   For example, having made a choice between two equally attractive sources of satisfaction or courses of action, the unattractive features of the rejected alternatives are systematically reinforced and its attractive features ignored, until what once represented a seductive choice is made to seem a wisely avoided mistake (Festinger 1957).

from the rest as the right number emerges unmistakeably from the confusion of dots on the optician's card. The presence of these people in our lives represents a meaning and purpose that we alone can distinguish; a world-pattern which is unique to ourselves, which other people cannot possibly understand because they cannot see it. The death of one of these vitally significant people shatters the entire pattern, and at the very moment when we need to depend upon its clear-sightedness, the rest of the world reveals itself as fatally colour blind.

This state of disruption and confusion which affects every aspect of life, every kind of perception, excites a longing for the restoration of order, because without order there can be neither meaning nor value, neither the possibility of rest nor the challenge to action. Without order, there can be no purpose, either in changing things or keeping them the same. Religion may be regarded as both a source of and a symbol of an essential order; and such is the nature of the pre-eminence of orderliness in the hierarchy of human mental needs, that the implication of the *possibility* or order makes religious symbols a source of the deepest comfort to existentially disturbed people. It is a commonplace among theologians that such religious symbols are, for believers, not simply descriptive but prescriptive, not only images of a religious reality but a way of importing that reality into the present situation.[3] It is perhaps worth saying, however, that in the presence of death, the most urgent existential crisis of all, such symbols become meaningful even for the non-religious, an alien or rejected meaning being preferable to no meaning at all.

Religion answers a need for meaning, order, purpose; but it is not itself that need. The assertion of explicit religious belief is the normative cultural expression of the struggle to achieve meaning in the face of death; but it is not the only way in which meaning may be asserted. There is a basic desire for meaning, associated with, and expressing itself in, a way of creating meaning which precedes any articulated religious doctrine about a postulated divine integrity. The ground for theology is already prepared by the existence of a mode of believing which precedes having anything to believe in: precedes it, suggests it and endeavours to create it. Religious belief is not imported into a situation of existential breakdown 'from the outside' as it were, as an ambulance is rushed into a disaster area to rescue the victims; it is one expression of a kind of thinking which is in fact characteristic of human mental processes, but which we become more than usually aware of in situations of existential challenge – situations which seem to put the fact of existence itself in question; situations of extreme personal and social trauma.

---

3   The proposition has come to be accepted by some cultural anthropologists as well. Cf. Geertz in Banton (ed) (1966).

It might, of course, be claimed that such thinking is really religious, in that it is the presupposition for religious belief in a transcendent source and expression of meaning, the human hunger which in the final event only God can satisfy. But it is not religious in the sense of being any kind of formulation about ultimate reality. It has more to do with the establishment and maintenance of a sense of personal identity, a trustworthy appreciation of one's meaning as a person, than with the willingness or ability to make definite statements about the character of divine personages, or even about their existence for that matter. The urge towards meaning serves an extremely practical end in bringing together separate, even disparate elements within the personality. It is the source of the interior movement to reconcile all kinds of experience of the self and other people, ways of behaving and reacting to familiar and unfamiliar situations, and to integrate them into a personality structure which is both representative and truthful—one that refuses to disown its own inclinations, whether these appear to it to be honourable or unworthy, and faces up to the mixed character of the motives that prompt most of its behaviour towards others and itself.[4]

This, of course, brings us out of the sphere of religion as such and into that of psychology and even psychiatry. We are concerned not with sanctity but sanity, although it may be that the first can only be properly established on the basis of the second. This is not of course to discount the part played by religious belief in helping the self to accept itself, to see its own interior conflicts as comprehended and reconciled from outside as it were; this is the effect of sanctity upon the self which is striving for sanity. Indeed, at the level of actual mental illness, the search for meaning is at its most unbearably intense, as anyone knows who has had much to do with patients suffering from clinical depression, or examined the paintings of schizophrenics and wondered at the overpowering minuteness of detail, the desperate urge to 'get everything in and make it all balance'. It is the threat of this kind of structural collapse and consequent total disintegration of the self that hangs over people whose personal world has received what seems to them to be the kind of blow from which it cannot ever recover. The only belief we are concerned with at this level of experience is a basic trust in the dignity and importance of being human. The *meaning* of being human. In the event, it is unlikely that the catastrophe which has befallen the bereaved person will have the effect of making him or her ill in the medical sense; although, of course, in certain circumstances this can happen. All the same, this is definitely the kind of thing that the death of a beloved person suggests to the mind of the bereaved.

4   Cf. Kelly (1963). Kelly has built up an entire theory of human personality on the fundamental postulate that, 'a person's processes are psychologically channelized by the ways in which they anticipate events' (p.46). Each of us possesses our own system for getting a grasp on things. Because our systems are flexible ('permeable'), they are always changing as we look for new ways of achieving order and balance in our experience of the world.

First and foremost, funeral rituals are important to the bereaved as a source of meaning. In this their significance is fundamental and belongs primarily not to what we know but to the way in which we know it. The rite itself is the action of shaping, of forming sense out of nonsense. It may have a religious message and provide a vehicle for definite teaching about personal survival; but above and beyond anything else it will be the symbol of an unspoken belief in personal *value*. To this extent it possessed an inalienably religious identity. What we are principally concerned with is not 'religion used to give meaning to death', but 'death used to reveal the meaning of life'. The action of burying or cremating the dead with ceremony imports its own meaning into existence.

It is able to do this because it is an assertion of belief in meaning. And what it asserts, it establishes. In symbolic ritual, we reach out into the unknown and integrate what we find there, integrate the *unknownness*, into the sum of our present knowledge. We have said that the rite 'makes sense out of nonsense'. It is always a particular kind of sense – sense which acknowledges the presence of nonsense, of the unknowable, the unassimilable. In the funeral rite, life and death, the known and the unknowable, come together as a symbol of human meaning. They belong together as a parable of the truth of personal experience, of the 'sadness in the sweet – And sweetness in the sad'. They express the central fact about being human: that to be alive is to discover an unanswered question at the heart of every conclusion. The rite is itself a declaration about open-endedness *because of* its identity as symbol. The factual reality of the symbol transmits a meaning which perceptually escapes it. Thus it rescues the possibility of meaning from the presence of meaninglessness, and by the action of reaching out transforms an absence into a kind of presence. Even to register meaninglessness is to transform its nature, to give it a kind of formal significance; to locate it within a scheme of proclaimed human purposes and values which then become all the more valuable and purposeful because of, and not in spite of, it. It is to produce an image of triumphant life, life in the presence of death – life out of death!

What I am doing here is simply describing a happening. I do not intend to preach any particular religious doctrine, merely to point out that mankind's recognition of the aesthetic process according to which newness and life are imaged forth by the action of proclaiming death as death, the essential precondition of renewal and rebirth, is available as evidence in support of a doctrine about the nature of a reality which is transcendent, as well as immanent. In other words, the triumph of meaning as it moves outwards from disaster and chaos may be considered to be a religious fact or a psychological one, a message from God or an attempt to distinguish a principle in the organisation of ongoing human experience. Whichever view we take, however, we must recognise that human experience, in order to qualify for the adjective 'human', must include self-conscious awareness of its own purposiveness. Human beings regard themselves as people engaged in making some kind of progress. The more difficult it is to make progress, the more satisfying the progress made. A self-ordering and self-perpetuating principle does exist. We move onwards *because* of the obstacles we perpetually discover in our path and not in spite of them.

The mind's innate tendency to 'conjure its own meanings' suggests that problems are not avoided as much as welcomed. Thus it is not to be regarded as being on the defensive so much as actually searching for the problems which alone offer it the opportunity to grow. The corollary is that our psychological *modus vivendi* demands that the projects we undertake be somehow or other carried to conclusion. If we are thwarted in our intentions we experience psychological discomfort in proportion to the degree with which we happen to have cherished a particular object. We put this discomfort to good use, as it intensifies our eagerness to find a solution to the problem which faces us, and when we find the answer we experience satisfaction. We do not rest here, of course; we must find new problems to solve, because the satisfaction of working on a problem turns out to be greater than that of arriving at a solution. There is no doubt that in certain cases and with some people the inability to reach satisfactory conclusions may result in *too much* anxiety, so that they either give up the struggle too early or begin to compensate by enjoying their failure too much, and end by actually preferring failure to success. It is in fact the overcoming of difficulties that we find pleasurable, not the presence either of difficulties or solutions. Modern investigation into the way the human brain functions reveals it as a problem-solving mechanism. Not merely a mechanism that can solve problems, but one that does solve them, and goes on doing so whenever it has the chance because it enjoys doing so. In other words, we are explorers, valuing new experience for its own sake. It is a sign that we are alive. We have a journey to make, and the more difficult the terrain, the greater the sense of achievement when we arrive at our destination.

In fact, what awaits us at the end of our journey is really of secondary importance to us. We will enjoy it when we get there. At the moment our satisfaction comes from 'travelling hopefully'. There is no question at all that we attach much higher value to painful experience, to goals achieved at some cost to ourselves, than we do to easy joys. This is particularly true about things we consider really important: our attitude to ourselves and other people, the parameters of our sense of identity, what the world is and who we are. An experiment carried out in America with university students (Aronson and Mills 1953, pp.119–124) suggested that people are much more eager to achieve a particular social status when this involves a certain definite effort, and even a degree of pain, than they are if the goal is offered to them at no cost to themselves. The purpose of setting up a situation to 'test the effect of severity of initiation upon liking for a group' and carrying the project through under the most rigorously controlled conditions, was simply to demonstrate scientifically what people have always known existentially; but it is interesting to know that the tendency is actually identifiable by means of psychological testing, nevertheless.[5]

In a well-known attempt to arrive at a typology of human attitudes to life itself, Spranger (1928) distinguished between the 'theoretical value' which concentrates upon the importance of knowledge and dependence on the tested and proven, and the 'aesthetic value', which leads people to judge according to the shape of actions or ideas, their appropriateness as a means of expression. Other values recognised by Spranger were the 'economic value' (the value of practicality), the 'social value' (which considers relationship with others to be of prime importance), the 'political value' (which has regard to power over the environment) and the 'religious value' (which looks outside what is immediately given and derives meaning from a metaphysical unity). Spranger points out that all these values play a part in influencing people in their behaviour and attitude to life. Some people are more inclined to be guided by one value than by another, and some kinds of action have a more definite relation to one than they do to another. Using Spranger's typology, the action of ceremonially disposing of the dead belongs obviously enough to 'religious value', as it is always an explicit expression of religious beliefs, wherever such beliefs are held.

However, the fact that it also takes place where they are not held and is instituted with a good deal of determination by people who are either non-religious by inclination or habit of mind, or whose adherence to any definite religious belief system is only nominal, prompts us to look for other value orientations which might be supposed to reinforce the religious one. The 'economic value' of funeralisation has often been written about; and there is no doubt that at certain times and in certain places funerals have been used to 'impress the neighbours' and so gain useful social prestige. The book that immediately springs to mind is of course Jessica Mitford's *The American Way of Death* (1963), but a similar situation has also been well described with regard to nineteenth-century England and France by Puckle (1926) and also by Habenstein and Lamers (1963). In *The High Cost of Dying*, which also concerns the twentieth-century American attitude to funerals, Ruth Mulvey Harmer (1963) suggested that people who had little influence in life sought to gain posthumous prestige by the magnificence of their own funeral, which might be quoted as an example of the 'political value' of funeralisation. The most powerful secondary value of all is certainly the 'aesthetic' one, the desire for order, balance and

5   Elliot Aronson and Judson Mills, in Cartwright and Zander (1953, pp.119–24). The same might be said of Zeigarnick's laboratory demonstration of subjects' 'tendency to return to incomplete tasks'. Funeral imagery provides many instances of the celebrated 'Zeigarnick effect'!

because it is one of the motives which turns men and women to religion at times of crisis, as well as being an expression of 'social value', the necessity of consolidating human relationships in a situation of collapse and incipient social disintegration.[6]

One of the more recent investigators into pathological mourning reaction, Colin Murray Parkes (1972), has reversed the general tendency among psychoanalytically orientated writers by being more concerned to show the importance of understanding what has happened to the conscious awareness of bereaved people than to theorise about their unconscious life (see, for example, Parkes 1964, 1965, 1972). Dr Parkes gives greater importance to the process of a conscious searching for an integrated understanding and a balanced awareness of an individual's present outlook than he does to the legacy of events which occurred, or may have occurred, in his long-past psychic life-history. In this he is supported by the sociologist, Dr Peter Marris.

There is reason to believe that the shock sustained by consciousness itself on the death of a dearly loved person is quite enough to cause the bereaved individual the very deepest mental anguish. There is no need to call upon 'the unconscious' in order to explain the violence of grief. Even that celebrated argument in support of unconscious motivation – the presence of feelings of guilt in bereaved people – may in fact have more to do with the ego than the id, for it may be traceable to the need to behave in a logical and operational way at a time when such behaviour is impossible. Indeed, according to the existentialist school of psychiatrists, Freud gravely underestimated the force and determination of the conscious mind in its search for meaning.

Professor Viktor Frankl certainly takes this view. The techniques of 'logotherapy', the name given by Dr Frankl and his associates to their particular approach to psychotherapy, are concerned with encouraging the disturbed and disorientated individual in his search for conscious meaning and purpose in the face of every kind of discouragement. 'Man', says Dr Frankl 'is ready to suffer if only he can be satisfied that his suffering has a meaning,' for 'the striving to find a

6   In fact, psychologists have claimed that religious belief does not really allay grief, although it certainly affects its quality. Specifically, it helps to counter tendencies towards psychological denial (cf. Sylvia Anthony, *The Child's Discovery of Death* (1940)). Alexander and Adlerstein, investigating anxiety about death in matching groups of religiously and non-religiously orientated students, came to the conclusion that, 'death anxiety is by no means dissipated by a religious approach to life' (1958, quoted in Kastenbaum and Aisenberg 1974, p.88). Earlier memories involving death are recalled more easily by religious people, but on the other hand the religious tend to be more alarmed by the prospect of their own dying. The religious, it seems, have a better grasp of the reality of death. Among non-religious people the usual defence is repression; but religion seems to make it easier for people to accept the factual presence of death – which is why the thought of their own dying is more terrifying to *them*.

only he can be satisfied that his suffering has a meaning,' for 'the striving to find a meaning in life is a primary motivational force in man' (1973, pp.34, 30). Frankl does not deny the Freudian 'pleasure principle' and the Adlerian 'will to power' as motivational forces. He simply says that both these impulses are symptomatic of a movement of the whole person towards a way of being which at present evades our grasp. They are not the result of repressed selfishness expressing itself at others' expense. On the contrary, they are to be seen as signs of an over-riding intention to transcend the self in an outward movement of the human soul which is truly other-directed.

Only the conscious awareness of human beings can entertain such an ideal. Only men and women possess the capability to subordinate the biologically determined homeostatic desire for satisfaction in the present to the idea of a richer and more satisfying, more complete fulfilment which can only be attained in the future. Certainly only men and women possess the faculty of positing a quality of satisfaction so very different from that which is currently available to their nervous system, and which possesses its ability to sustain and uplift precisely because it is so different, so far outside their animal experience. The search for meaning, like the search for pleasure and the urge for dominance, is the product of an environment which causes frustration, but what is frustrated here is not an unconscious libidinal instinct aiming at its own release and satisfaction, but a consciously willed intention directing itself towards a quality of experience not yet attained, which stands over against the self as an unknown perfection of being, calling us perpetually to itself and ourselves.

Writing as a psychologist and psychiatrist, and not as a theologian, Frankl nevertheless claims that effective psychotherapy must be founded on the admission that in order to find his true self, man must aim higher than himself, moving outwards beyond himself towards a source of complete meaning. Meaning must not merely be acknowledged, it must be fulfilled; and by giving himself to the action and intention of searching out and following up his own vision of his personal meaning, men and women fulfil thier proper destiny. In psychological terms, they move towards the eventual integration of their own personalities. In searching we find ourselves; our identity reveals itself in terms of our destiny. We know ourselves in terms of the task we have taken in hand, for we are not finders but searchers.' (Frankl 1973, p.31). Like iron filings in magnetic field, man's life is put in order through his orientation towards meaning.' Whatever we encounter in this journey, whether discouragement or encouragement, serves only to define the direction we must take. Both clarity and confusion point to the existence of a meaning towards which a primal orientation drives us onwards.

A determination to make use of all the experiences of life, whether they are positive or negative, obstacles or invitations, as so many signposts towards an ideal way of living is, we are told, a characteristic of the human species as a whole. This is the judgment of anthropologists and psychologists. It is a religious instinct insofar as it represents the human side of the religious universe which is posited by the faith of believers. Thus it is the discernible aspect of religion. Indeed, as far as sociological and psychological observers are concerned it *is* religion. Religion is the urge to discover ideal answers to existential questions; and theology exists to provide such answers. Criticism of the quality of the answers provided is not incompatible with acknowledgement of the fact that there are essential questions to be asked, questions concerned with the final meaning of existence, and that to ask them, and to go on asking them, is natural to human beings.

What we are concerned with here is something outside the scientific universe, however. It is the satisfaction which belongs to the asking of unanswerable questions which is intrinsic to the religious search itself. Any accurate account of the religious impulse must give due weight to this key factor in religious experience. In their own ways, both anthropology and psychopathology reduce the integrative role of religion in bereavement to the simple re-establishment of the psycho-social status quo which existed before death occurred. This reveals a fundamental misunderstanding of the nature and quality of religious awareness. The idea of an achievable norm with regard to life itself is a distortion of human reality. The satisfaction which men and women search after is always an idealised completeness, never simply the restoration of tangible satisfactions. At the very least it is the desire for a state of affairs in which past joys will be made present in a new way, flawlessly present, always present. Experience is to be recapitulated in its idealised essence, rescued forever from transitoriness and the flux of time. Thus the meaning that men and women spend their lives searching for evades them, whether they seek it in the past or the future. The searching is the living.

This is the distinctive quality of human life and these are the terms according to which human life is *enjoyed*. If we were concerned merely to isolate some kind of impersonal 'psychic energy' which motivated us and explained our way of looking at life, then a conceptual model showing the purpose of human existence as the kind of static satisfaction brought about by the balancing out of psychological needs would be adequate for our purpose. We have reason to believe that this is not, in fact, the way in which the mind works; and an ever-increasing body of experimental research adds weight to our supposition that human beings live by the interchange, not of simple energy, but of organised knowledge – of a communicated awareness of ideas and of *ideation*, whose purpose is the arranging and processing of information for future use, in order to improve the past and not merely reproduce it. Any model of mental mechanisms must therefore be an open-ended one. The symbolic nature of our mental constructs demands that we recognise that our attempts to describe the workings of our minds, the pictures we draw of our own action and reactions, must also be they live. As far as we are concerned, meaning itself demands the perpetual elaboration of systems rather than the construction of a static and inclusive 'final system'. Whatever Freud may have to say on the matter, the mind's characteristic orientation is not towards homeostatic repose, but to the accommodation of manageable problems, a health human 'mental set' containing within itself the presence of the asystematic and asymmetric. The exchange of energy which we call human being is directed towards, not the *absence* of difficulties and obstructions, but their presence. We search for the grit which will produce the pearl for us.[7]

The mind, then, is a problem-solving mechanism which thrives on the challenges involved in dealing with difficulties. With this in view, we can take a closer look at the role of religion in human behaviour. This involves us making a distinction, however, between religious *faith* and religious *dogma*. Religious dogma is an attempt to answer certain basic questions about life in the world. The acceptance of religious explanations delivers the believer from doubt and uncertainty. As far as this goes, it is a satisfactory account of the psycho-social function of religion. As an explanation of the experiential truth of religion, it is inadequate, however. How does dogma perform this function? The reasons it supplies often seem rather likely! How is the 'religious' person or society able to accept the far-fetched assurance of doctrine? A functional explanation of religion takes no account of faith. Faith, the basic trust in a transcendent goodness, purpose and meaning, attacks disbelief and scepticism simultaneously on two fronts. It provides the ability to accept 'unlikely' answers to existential questions, a fact that has frequently been pointed out before. However, it does something equally important as well.

A faithful person, one who lives in the consciousness of a personal relationship with God, finds that he has a certain ability to exercise what might be called 'cognitive discretion'. He does not press existential questions too far or examine official answers too minutely. He is willing to wait and see. Religious faith is the ability to live in the presence of unanswered questions, as well as the thing that encourages us to go on asking questions. It is an ability to tolerate existential negativity because of a primary assurance of existential positivity. Its essential congruity with the facts of thinking, the way in which the human mind works, is the ground of its genuine plausibility. As with the processes of thinking, so with

7   This description of mental mechanism owes a good deal to the 'learning theory' school of developmental psychology, and particularly to the 'cognitive developmental' approach of Piaget and Kohlberg, which suggests a process of interaction between the discovery of new information and the developing ability of the mind to make use of such information in building an expanding view of reality. Such a model of human cognition is the premise on which Personal Construct Psychology adn Gestalt Therapy are founded (cf. Kelly 1963 and Perls, Hefferline and Goodman 1973).

the ground of its genuine plausibility. As with the processes of thinking, so with the experience of faith: difficulties and problems, whether they are behavioural, intellectual or emotional, are grist to its mill. Like the normal mental activity of healthy people, it is not content to achieve a condition of stasis, but works towards the elaboration of creative patterns. Its action is aesthetic, in that it images forth an expanding succession of pregnant conclusions. Even death itself, the shattering of all existential unity, is not simply denied but used for the purpose of achieving a greater wholeness of vision. The ideas in which this spiritual mastery are communicated are the story-forms of myth. The language used is the language of the rite. Through its mythical scenario the funeral rite embraces death.

The rite embraces death. The rite is not an argument, though. It is a gesture. A gesture of immense corporate and personal significance, but a gesture all the same. It is not a teaching mechanism, despite the propositional form of its mystical scenario. It does not explain, it expresses. Its form is the action of homologising death with the events of life. We pass through death into life in company with a mythical hero or according to a divine plan made on our behalf. Its essential significance is the significance of the symbol. Perhaps a good way of putting it would be to say that it is not a factual account but a potent story; not factual, that is, in any way that is open to experimental testing, although it may well be in strict conformity to the facts of faith. The rite accepts death by the action of confronting it and expressing a faithful dis-belief in its finality. In its attempts to deal with 'the marginal situation par excellence' (Berger 1973, p.32), the passage rite is revealed as no social formula but a genuine religious symbol, open-ended, propositionally inclusive, the dramatic confrontation between knowledge in its most implacable and intransigent, its most *final* form – and faith. Rites of passage are ways of facing up to existential problems by what Douglas has called the expression of a well formed wish in the belief that such a wish calls forth a response in the mind and heart of God (1966 pp.63, 64).

The greatest problem that ever faces us is the problem of death, whether it be someone else's or our own. It is consequently the greatest test of all of our ability to make use of pain, to take the problem into the system and learn from the experience of doing so. Religious belief about personal survival provides us with immense support because it reassures us about the extrinsic value of what is happening, the objective purpose of our journeying through bereavement or through the experience of death itself. It offers a glimpse of the landscape which awaits our gaze on the other side of the frontier. But our attitude to death as something possessing intrinsic value for us, something we can make use of as a way of increasing the value of our personal offering to life, our individual existential gesture, is a factor in the situation which is of equal importance.

And so we return to Antigone's gesture in demanding a 'proper' funeral for Polynices. It would not be accurate to say that Antigone, even Anouilh's Antigone, she gives her own life to provide. Nevertheless, she is motivated much more powerfully by an intrinsic sense of rightness. Death does not lose its existential significance or become a purely negative event; as with the specifically religious view of dying, it appears as a springboard into a fuller and richer kind of living; one which is more honest, more realistic, more accepting, more aware. The awareness of the reality of death, its final and uncompromising nature as an event outside life (to use Wittgenstein's phrase) heightens the significance of living human gestures, those actions which proclaim a belief in the innate value of being human and being alive.

We have good reason to believe that funeral rituals provide a symbolic function of the very greatest importance, both for individuals and for groups. Their use is both therapeutic and structural; they are therapeutic *because* they are structural. These rituals, or ritual matrices, locate death by their ability to say something definite about it. What they have to say is decided in and by the saying, so that the action of performing them is itself therapeutic and significant. It is therapeutic because it is significant, and significant because it is shapely. In the presence of death *shapeliness*, significant form, is the longed-for element, both in the experience of the individual and that of the group. The ritual complex answers its own question in the action of giving form to the question, the form of an open-ended symbol, and it is able to do this because the question is principally a question *about* form.

In the typical funeral rite, form is given to the disparate elements which make up the grief reaction of individuals and groups. This is done by a process of containment. In fact, the funeral rite reproduces the shape of death. 'In these plastic dramas,' says the cultural anthropologist, Clifford Geertz, 'men attain their faith as they portray it'(1966, p.29) The faith that is attained is first and foremost faith in the meaning of making gestures of affirmation, of countering the sense of meaninglessness with a demonstration of the human ability to create forms even in the experience of chaos – to create them out of that experience. The rite is not primarily an argument or a discourse, either about God or man, but a happening. In this basic identity it is a proclamation of meaning, an outburst of life, which, in Shelley's words, 'Like a dome of many-coloured glass, stains the white radiance of Eternity.'

It is not difficult to see how a mechanism which creates a sense of form, and consequently a feeling of value and human purpose, will have a direct application to the condition of human grieving. The conflicts which so many writers have described as being central to the state of grieving signify a loss of meaning of immense proportions. The 'grief work' described by Freud (1917) is nothing less than the re-construction of a meaningful personal universe. The widows of Marris' classic study were observed as being involved in the task of adjusting not only to the loss of their husbands, but also to the loss of themselves (1958). The study of funeral rituals throughout the world reveals that the actual shape of funerals has a tendency to conform to the outline of this process of existential reconstruction. The expressive function of all ritual action has often been remarked upon, and rites and ceremonies are commonly explained as ways of bring about a catharsis of sympathetic emotion, particularly so when the actions involved correspond more or less accurately to the overall emotional state of those taking part in them. Their formal significance, by which is meant their identity as diagrams of existential states, has not often been distinguished. Peter Bond, however, writing in 1970, says that, 'ceremony in its broadest sense involves a series of movements, actions and words which, together with the environment in which they take place, form a complete and significant pattern. A person experiencing this pattern,' he says, 'should find in it a correspondence to the feelings which move him at the time. The degree to which this correspondence is achieved will determine the extent to which a person will be able to find expression for his feelings, and the degree to which he is fulfilled'.[8]

Mr Bond is an architect, and he is writing on the subject of the architectural setting of funeral services. But the principle he sets out here has been recognised and remarked upon by sociologists and anthropologists, historians of religion and other students of ritual – and even, from time to time, by theologians! Writing from the point of view of a medical investigator into the processes of grief and mourning, Dr Robert Hobson is even more specific about the relationship between ritual and grieving, and draws a parallel between the three-fold shape of the classic rite of passage and the outline of the mourning process itself as this has been described by a whole succession of observers: 'a comparative cross-cultural study of death rites reveals a sequence of three stages, separation, transition and re-incorporation which roughly corresponds to the three phases of individual mourning', which he distinguishes as 'shock', 'disorganisation' and 're-organisation' (1970, p.472). In *Death, Grief and Mourning*, Geoffrey Gorer maintains that the universal provenance of the tripartite rite of passage as a way of dealing with bereavement is evidence that there is a correspondence between the natural course of grieving and the succession of stages or movements within the rite itself. Gorer identifies the stages of grief in much the same way as Dr Hobson:

> a short period of shock, usually between the occurrence of death and the disposal of the body; [followed by] a period of intense mourning, accompanied by withdrawal of much attention from the external world, and by such psychological changes as disturbed and restless sleep, often with vivid dreams, failure of appetite and loss of weight; a final period of re-established physical

8   Included in Cope (1970, p.88).

homeostasis, sleep and weight again established, interest again directed outwards.' (1965, p.112)

These stages in bereavement correspond to the three sub-categories of the rite of passage: the rites of *separation, transition* and *incorporation* (what Van Gennep (1965, p.11) calls 'pre-liminal, liminal and post-liminal rites'). Funeral rites may be divided into a pre-liminal movement or ceremony of dismissal; a liminal stage of median chaos or formlessness, characterised by the anarchic expression of rebellious feelings; and a post-liminal movement of reintegration. As we have seen, a survey of the funeral behaviour of various cultures and peoples does in fact reveal the presence of these three motifs, whether they are contained within the framework of one ceremony or are divided from one another by an interval of time, so that they resemble the three distinct rites, or groups of rites, described by Van Gennep.

This element of what we might call 'developmental triplicity' is of the greatest importance. It is at one and the same time the shape of mourning and the shape taken by these ceremonies which celebrate the salient facts about the religious view of dying: that the dead person, first of all, leaves his old home, then passes through a period of radical change, then arrives at, or is admitted into, his new condition of life. The homologisation of the facts of the experience of bereavement with the religious message of the rite has a homeopathic force which cannot be overlooked and is vouched for by anthropologists. Just as life itself, in its inner religious significance, passes out of a limited and dependent condition, through an essential middle period of change, into the state of radical renewal and the final and total release from every sort of limitation, so the stricken mourner will experience the resurgence of his own ability to 'be himself' once again and to enjoy a new quality of life, having gained spiritually from an ordeal which he has endured and yet survived. Gorer (1965), Marris (1958) and others have remarked on the loss of psychological comfort to the bereaved which has resulted from letting the detailed and comprehensive funeral rites of previous generations fall into disuse in Western Europe, and particularly in Britain; and Solon Kimball has claimed that the general neglect of rites of passage as a way of expressing and enabling psycho-social development in times of crucial change in the lives of individuals may actually be a cause of mental and emotional breakdown.[9]

---

9   'The critical problems of becoming male and female, of relations within the family and of passing into old age are directly related to the devices which society offers the individual to help him achieve the new adjustment ... it seems likely that one dimension of mental illness may arise because an increasing number of individuals are forced to accomplish their transitions alone with private symbols' (S. Kimball, Introduction to Van Gennep's *Rites of Passage* (1965, pp.xvii, xviii)).

Perhaps we might pause here to consider the exact nature of this 'homeopathic force' possessed by the three-fold rite of passage, with particular reference to its use as a funeral ceremony. The three sections of the rite provide a kind of picture of the experience of grieving. In the pre-liminal section the element of shock is mirrored in the presence of various motifs of dismissal and abandonment of the dead by the living: the obsession with discontinuity is signalled by the action of disposal of the body itself and its attendant imagery of journeying and departure which is reinforced in some cultures by the burning of a person's house, the destruction of his possessions, even the dismemberment and abuse of his corpse – all of them images of destruction and collapse of a radical nature, things too awful to contemplate which must nevertheless be contemplated. The central section of the rite depicts with varying degrees of clarity the ensuing existential turmoil, both in individuals and societies, typified by the funeral wake, but symbolically present in a whole range of 'abnormal' procedures, reversals of ordinary social practice, outbursts of violence, either actual or mimic, at the expense of oneself and other people. Out of this chaotic middle section there gradually emerges, as the cosmogenising principle which guides human activities asserts itself again, a state of reorganisation which is proclaimed and established in a post-liminal rite at which the dead are welcomed back into the life of the living and, by implication, into the conscious awareness of the bereaved themselves.

Funeral rituals throughout the world possess this pictorial quality, although the particular motifs which make up the total picture – motifs of dismissal, disintegration and restoration of wholeness – do not always occur in sequence. This applies in particular to those which related to the central idea of re-generative chaos, which frequently refer both backwards and forwards, and possess a symbolic quality of resonance which refuses to be kept within schematic limits. For example, the wake-feast may be held either after interment (its usual location) or before it. In the latter instance it takes place in the presence of the corpse, which serves both as a memorial of times past and a gesture of continuity, a determination to include the dead man in whatever is happening, an expression of an underlying belief in the renewal of life even in the midst of chaos. The body always seems to have this dual significance, as Malinowski (1974) points out: even where the flesh is stripped from the bones, the skeleton is preserved as a pledge of future hope. The exact nature of this hope, its propositional content, is not always spelled out in an orderly succession of ritual 'diagrams', nor do the various movements of the ritual complex always coincide exactly with the progress of the psychological grief reaction, for they are often telescoped together into a comparatively short period of time, much shorter than the recovery period which is considered normal for bereaved people and which may extend into a period of years rather than months. Even so, the ritual may be therapeutically valuable for this very reason, as it helps to concentrate the work of grieving, in much the same way that group therapy contrives to short-circuit the more lengthy processes of individual analysis. The funeral serves to intensify feelings to the degree at which they can no longer be hidden or denied, to force them to be expressed so that they may be lived through within a supportive environment. The result may be a kind of 'psychological flooding' of the kind advocated by some clinical psychologists.

In much the same way, the stages of grief in bereaved people are not divisible into three convenient sections. Dr Murray Parkes (1972), for example, distinguishes four 'clinical pictures' which blend into and replace one another: numbness, pining, depression and recovery.[10] However, insofar as grieving is a process which must somehow be 'worked through' by the bereaved person – and almost every writer on the subject agrees that this is the case – its course must conform to a basic three-fold scheme. In other words, it must have a beginning, a middle and an end. It appears that in processes which concern the reaction of people and animals to an experience of a violently traumatic kind, these three sections tend to be very clearly defined, as they are in Caplan's descriptions of human reaction to crisis situations of all kinds (1964). The 'shock/confusion/reintegration' pattern of behaviour seems the inevitable reaction to violent happenings affecting the life-career of individuals and the social organisation of groups. To this extent, then, the rite of passage certainly mirrors the actual experience of the bereaved.

In some cultures, where the three parts of the funeral complex are strongly differentiated and quite clearly defined, the rite itself, because of this pictorial quality, is able to give form to the experience of bereavement, and to concentrate the work of grieving by providing a kind of religious commentary upon it. A very good example of this would be the traditional procedure in Roman Catholic countries, where the ceremony of interment is followed by a funeral meal which may be either more or less restrained but is associated with the provision of social and family support for the bereaved during the height of their grieving, and the dead person is remembered (and in a sense recalled) in a series of Requiem Masses held at intervals during the succeeding months. The practice is not confined to Roman Catholic Christians, however. Among the Armenian Orthodox, for example, the dead person's grave is always visited on the eighth and fortieth days after the funeral, and then every year afterwards, in addition to a ceremonial visit on the day following each of the five great Church festivals (Davies and George 1965, p.43). Many cultures throughout the world actually allow their dead a

10   Some commentators refer to *stages* of grief, others to *components*. In our experience there is a sequential character to the process, but with so much 'regression' to earlier stages that it may be better to use the term 'components' and qualify it by saying that some components predominate early in the process and others at a later stage. For example, denial and despair are common in the early period of loss and aggression is rare; later, aggression may be prominent but with frequent lapses into denial and depression.

second, final funeral, which is accepted as marking the end of an interim period of intensive personal and social mourning. Among the Todas, for example, this service takes place a year after the first one, the bones being preserved during the interval in a special hut reserved for the purpose (Habenstein and Lamers 1963, p.140).

Similarly, many cultures have a way of phasing out mourning by laying down set times at which ceremonies of remembrance and recognition are to take place. These usually occur at greater intervals throughout the months following bereavement, and are often renewed on one occasion each year, usually on the anniversary of the death itself. In this way, the intensity of ritual activity reproduces the downward scale of the intensity of mourning, setting a limit to socially recognised grieving but not to remembrance. In this way also, the bereaved are given a definite task to perform: the established ceremonial recognition of a loved person's death, which often has the effect of lessening the terrible feeling of helpless frustration that 'there is nothing that I or anybody else can do'. When, in the course of time, they become aware of a lessening in the intensity of their grieving, the process of emerging into a more normal way of living and a quieter and more accepting state of mind is publicly recognised and they are encouraged in the feeling that they have 'done all they can'. The assurances of friends that it is time to 'get on with the business of living' and that the dead person 'would not want you to go on like this' begin to make a bit more sense than they have been doing.[11]

Thus the ritual complex is able to provide the bereaved with an articulated scenario of the process of mourning, and an opportunity to act out the various components or stages of emotional distress involved in the grief reaction, either in the contracted milieu of a single funeral ritual which contains all three motifs, or in an extended series of rites. There is, however, another significance inherent in

11   Bendann, Jones and Habenstein and Lamers give many examples of post-liminal funeral ceremonies and 'time-limiting mourning' (Gorer's phrase). At Waga Waga, according to Bendann, the dead person's family enjoy a series of feasts or *banahiva*, following one another at intervals of one or two months after the death: 'the last of these is similar to the first, but grander' (1930, p.147, 148). The Australian Koita have three principal feasts, two of them during the first week of bereavement and the third six months later, when the food restrictions binding upon mourners are finally lifted. The central feast is the most extended and the ritual wake activity more intensive, while the final one signifies the 'laying to rest' of active mourning (Bendann 1930, p.148). Lily Pincus describes an East African 'second funeral': 'If the dead person is a man, his son prepares an effigy of him. On the day of the anniversary of death the grave is slightly reopened and with much lamenting and grieving, the effigy is put on top of the body but facing in the opposite direction. This means that the dead man has now left the living world and joined his ancestors, and the surviving are free to live their own lives. His widows (there may be as many as four), who throughout the year have worn mourning cords around their waists, remarry, and their new husbands cut the cord at the grave. The atmosphere changes from mourning to rejoicing' (1976, pp.255, 256). Vide p.119, The Funeral Motif of Re-integration.

the three-fold nature of the passage rite, one which is different from its pictorial or homeopathic quality. This is what we might call the overall symbolic effect of the funeral, which is not one of *change* but of *finality*. It is, in fact, the finality which permits change, because it permits the possibility of something totally new. It cannot do this unless it establishes itself first of all as a kind of landmark, a fixed point in a world in flux. Its primary purpose here is to establish the factuality of death as something which must not be ignored or denied, for 'among all the ways of dealing with death, the one most surety doomed to failure is the attempt to ignore it'.[12] The extended three-fold ritual presents a vivid image of death, of inevitable disruption and chaos, and of the equally inevitable movement towards renewal. It is particularly vivid not only because of its literal quality, which makes it a kind of guided tour of death, but also because of its shape, which is the schema of all real existential change.

For real change, change of a vital and life-transforming nature, to take place, the old situation must really finish and the new one begin. For the new state of affairs to live, the old one must die. This means that of necessity there must be a crucial point in the dynamism of progression at which the old situation finishes and the new one begins, a pivotal moment upon which the dynamics of change depend, and around which the movement of change arranges itself. This moment has no dynamism of its own, belonging neither to what is finishing nor to what is beginning. And yet it belongs to both. When we think about change, we tend to overlook this central position. As A.B. Kempe (1890) says: 'It is characteristically human to think in terms of dyadic relations: we habitually break up a triadic relation into a pair of dyads'. In the case of a traumatic life experience, we think of ourselves as going out of the world of normality, the world of meaning, into a world of chaos and confusion; then, when we are beginning to recover from the experience, we are vaguely aware of a movement out of a state of distressful disorganisation into a more peaceful frame of mind. What we tend to overlook is that the chaos into which we are propelled and that from which we emerge is *the same chaos*.

The effectiveness of the rite as a prophylactic against the crippling effect of traumatic life experiences may well be that it states the importance of the central moment of change so clearly and dramatically. In the rite of passage all the circumstances of an existential revolution are made symbolically present in their entirety, without any glossing over of the central point of rest, that crucial phase of present being without which change is not change at all and we are caught between past and future, living in a fantasy world in which the past is about to happen and the future long since settled, and the mind moves backwards and forwards in the frantic world of wish-fulfilment whose only reality is the

12   C.N. Carstairs in Hinton (1967, p.8).

underlying presence of despair. The rite illustrates the preconditions of a real change, not just a mental leap. This is important with regard to death, the actual death of people we know and love, because the part of what is happening to us that we automatically hide is in fact the most painful part. When instinct and training urge us to leap over the tomb itself into a fantasy future, the rite brings us face to face with death and allows us to die, so that we may eventually live.

It is its three-fold nature that makes the rite *practical*. The rite of passage proposes that in order to get from one place to another we have to pass through the barrier that divides them. it makes us face this unpleasant fact by demonstrating it to us in a literal way, and then incorporating us in it. it is not simply that the fact of change is, to use Hamelin's word, 'historicised':[13] it is actually given a physical, geographical location. It uses the language of place to talk about time. It gives a quality of correctness and definition to moral decisions and movements of the soul. The passage from one existential position to another is identified with a territorial passage, such as the entrance into a village or a house, the movement from one room to another or the crossing of streets and squares. The tripartite experience is a basic anthropological sign language. We are presented with a grammar of change and progression, a kind of privileged mode of communication making possible the direct expression of feeling, the celebration of experience unclouded by the ambiguities of argument. We shall have more to say about the 'privileged' status of the rite in the next chapter.

The model of moral action is, of course, necessarily tripartite, as the choosing person considers a particular course of action and decides either for or against it. It might be argued that the interpersonal behaviour of men and women has the same shape, and that relationship itself 'possesses a triune image', as we relate to another within the context of all other possible relationships, against the background of the whole universe of personal responsibility, of what we call 'involvement' – a fact which erupts into our awareness from time to time when we are confronted by a familiar situation of 'the eternal triangle', in which the choosing agent sees the whole of his moral life in terms of a threatening and confining triad. However, even when this element of moral choice is taken away, the same basic alignment is revealed. We do not have to choose our relationships in this circumscribed and dramatic way. We are already in a wider and more inclusive relation with our environment. To be precise, we are aware of a responsibility to the natural world, to our fellows, and to that universe of meaning and value which governs our specifically human mode of regarding both the world and our fellow men and women. And this is man's necessary mode of being.[14]

---

13   'The essential point about Van Gennep's thesis is that it consists in showing that as far as rituals go, change is articulated in 3 stages' (Hamelin 1972, pp.133–43).

Within the self-contained model of change which is the basic shape of the rite, the climax or actual point of change occurs at the centre just as in a three-act play, the second act curtain is traditionally the most dramatic and suspenseful. Here the tripartite shape provides the possibility of a climactic *reversal*. But when the purpose of triplicity is to give particular emphasis to a proposition, or to mark the special significance of something that has happened or is about to happen, the climax occurs at the end. The three-fold rite of passage combines both these aspects of the triple statement. When such rites are used to celebrate an actual death (rather than a status change concerning an individual's ongoing life in this world), this second function is the dominant one. The funeral ritual emphasises the fact of death. Certainly it is a dying which carries with it the idea of change; nevertheless it is a death. This is the message which the funeral ritual must somehow deliver, and deliver as forcibly and dramatically as may be. In the three-fold rite, the information is transmitted three times, to make quite sure that it registers.

A succession of three happenings or stages represents the minimum needed to produce a climax. In the myths which underlie so many of the well-tried plots in formal and informal story-telling, the whole action depends on a question of three-ness. The hero has three wishes, must answer three riddles or defeat three monsters. The last wish is always more fatal, the last riddle more difficult to solve, the last monster more horrifyingly fierce, than either the first or the second. Three brothers compete for the hand of a princess and the socially least 'suitable' suitor wins her hand in marriage.[15] Above all, three is the number of clarity and

14   It is not possible adequately to explore the religious implications of 'threeness' here. Both Christianity and Hinduism are 'trinitarian' religions, as, in a slightly different sense, is Buddhism. The Bible is almost a textbook of 'tripartite change', with its accounts of geospiritual journeys concerning individuals, nations and tribes, as in the account of the Red Sea passage and the voyages of St Paul, or the human race as a whole, as with the story of Noah and, indeed, the entire Biblical narrative in its Christian version as the Creation, Fall and Restoration of man. The New Testament attitude to the 'three-fold living relation' of man (Buber's term) is clearly expressed in the account of Christ's temptations (Mtt. 4:1–11, Lk. 4:13), where satanic pressure is brought to bear on each of these essential relationships, as Christ is urged to misuse his divine authority with regard to his human relation to nature (Mtt. 4:3, 4, Lk. 4:3, 4), his fellow men (Mtt. 4: 8–10, Lk. 4: 5–8), and to God (Mtt. 4: 9–12, Lk. 4: 9–12). We might note that according to the trinitarian doctrine of Richard de St-Victor, love itself inevitably suggests and involves a three-fold interaction, as the love between God the Father and God the Son demands the presence of the Third Person of the Holy Trinity, 'for the essential ingredient of true charity is not merely to love the other as one is loved oneself and to be beloved in return, but to want the other to be loved as one is loved' (St-Victor 1959)

15   As in dramatic effect, so in humour. In his half-learned, half-instinctive manipulation of the audience, a comedian knows that he will get the most satisfactory reaction when he trips over his coat-tails for the third time in succession. The catchphrase which brought hardly a chuckle when it was said for the first time is greeted with rapture at its third appearance. At a less conscious level, Freud analysed the motives which underlie the universal image of the

definition. Everyone who is concerned to transmit ideas or pass on information by actual demonstration knows the value of the old saying beloved by actors and teachers: 'tell them you're going to do it; do it; then tell them you've done it'. The progression carries the idea of authority, the impression of conviction, of an understanding firmly held and efficiently hammered home. It is the model of a point well made.

In fact, it has been suggested that this formula may correspond to a well-defined neural function, and that it represents a kind of minimum requirement for authoritative reception of a new or difficult idea by the brain. As Norbert Weiner says:

> We can hardly expect that any important message is entrusted for transmission to a single neuron nor that any important operation is entrusted to a single neuronal mechanism. Like the computing machine, the brain probably works on a variant of the famous principle expounded by Lewis Carroll in *The Hunting of the Snark* – 'what I tell you three times is true.' (1948, pp.145–146)

What I am trying to say here is that, in fact, the cumulative effect of the funeral complex as a succession of assertions about the reality of death – either its objective theological reality or the subjective psychological reality of bereavement – is at least as important as the pictorial quality of the funeral scenario. Even when the rite is not in itself cumulative – that is, where it is not divisible into three separate though connected movements – it still contributes to an overall cumulative effect, for it is part of a triad of happenings which together constitute death as a real event and allow it to be assimilated by the mind: the death itself, the funeral and the work of mourning, and the process of working through and attaining a new kind of personal organisation, whether this takes a few months or several years.

It is the element of shape that gives meaning to a succession of happenings. Without this they remain merely a random assortment of heterogeneous data, the raw material of experience rather than experience itself. The catastrophic effect of bereavement, its identity as radical discontinuity – the actual presence within the experience of grieving of chaotic elements and symbols of disorganisation amounting to the dislocation of an entire lifestyle, the automatic rejection of what has happened, its utter existential impossibility – all render the achievement of some kind of shape critically necessary. Death and bereavement call out for something else that is real and salutary, for a third member of the essential transactional triad, to provide at least the possibility of unity and definition.

This 'third factor' is the funeral itself. In the traditional funeral, complex shape is organically present. The extended rite makes triply sure that death is not

fateful choice among three in *The Theme of the Three Caskets* (Freud 1913).

ignored and denied – we are *involved* by its three-dimensional symbolism of personal interaction, *convinced* by the conclusiveness of its three-fold repetition and *prepared* for the future by its articulation around a central point of change, the pivotal moment of reversal which lies at the heart of every corporate ceremony. In these ways the rite itself constitutes an effective symbol of the acceptance and subsequent ordering of existential chaos. Even where this is not the case, and the funeral is reduced to a single ceremony of farewell accompanying the actual disposal of the body, the ritual nature of this action gives it vital significance for the acceptance of reality and eventual reconstruction of meaning. What matters is not principally the three-ness of the rite itself, but the three-ness that the rite *permits*. The pictorial content serves the pivotal effect; the force of the symbol lies in its action as a catalyst, its ability to promote change by underlining reality.

The rite functions as a resolution of psychological conflict. A study of the actual working of religious ritual reveals that it is always concerned to hold opposing forces in tension. The rite aims at making a synthesis of oppositions. It brings together the world of men and the reality of the divine in a fruitful meeting, one which proves fruitful because of the difference between these two realities. This is the rite's honesty; it proclaims the relation between Man and God, present and future, the actual and the ideal, to be one of difference. By doing this it allows that relation to be a true relationship – not a confusion but an encounter, not the arrogation of an inauthentic parity but a reaching-out towards perfection. Mutuality is achieved in the action of reaching across, in the relational event. Thus the rite serves to bless men in their factual humanity, not to confirm them in a fantasised divinity in which they grasp omnipotence at the expense of God and one another. There is no confusion in the action of the rite, although the rite may contain confusion. There is no blurring of the outlines of self and other but a demonstration of the distance that divides, upon which relationship depends. Thus the confusion becomes part of the rite's honesty, its willingness to proclaim the facts of the case with regard to the human reality it presents, the difficulties to be overcome, the obstacles which stand between man and the object of his aspiration; the difficulties and obstacles which, in fact, are the motive power for aspiration. The rite must contain chaos, as in the context of divinity chaos is a part of simple human truth; and if relationship is to be achieved, truthfulness must be preserved.

Thus ritual and reconciliation go together. 'The rites and ceremonies of the Ovimbundo [W. Africa] are very social,' say Habenstein and Lamers, 'especially funerals and post-funeral rites … which make for the greatest social cohesion' (1963, p.258). Rituals implement that to which they aspire. As Max Gluckmann says, 'What Durkheim missed when he derived God from the feeling of the pressure of society at an Australian corroborree was that the members of the congregation assembled in unity there were enemies of one another in many other situations' (1962, pp.40–41). In the same book, V.W. Turner claims that rites function 'in order to overcome cleavages in society' (p.146). He draws special attention to the role of mortuary rituals in reconciling warring family interests among the Yako. Anthropologists who acknowledge the influence of Van Gennep upon their thinking have drawn attention to the unifying force of religious ritual, whereby the rite becomes a language capable of expressing opposing ideas and accommodating differences and contradictions within the framework of a comprehensive codification of experience. Thus religion and its rituals actively promote harmony and are not simply the expression or enactment of an existing unity and completion.

Sometimes the need for unity between the dead and the living reaches an intolerable climax. One reason for having a funeral is that, 'it builds a bridge between us, the living, and the silent totality in which most of mankind resides' (Weisman 1976 p.xiii). Perhaps the gap between life and death, the living and the dead, is most powerfully felt when the one who has died is a child. Bereaved people thank God for the memories they carry with them of the person who has died: 'It's all I've got now, isn't it?' When children die such memories are clung to even more intensely because there are not so many of them. In the case of perinatal death and stillbirth there are none at all. To have hardly lived may be considered to have scarcely died: as it says on an eighteenth-century child's grave: 'Came in, look'd out, Didn't like it, went out'. Went out: but when he went he left behind him such grief, such longing for what might have been, such anger towards God, such frustration towards life. We have no way of telling whether these feelings were ever expressed, whether they were turned inward upon the self or outward towards the world. Or simply denied. In the case of interrupted pregnancy and perinatal death a similar state of affairs is bound to exist, perhaps in some cases even more intensely. After carrying a growing child within oneself for nine months and thinking, feeling, planning, measuring, rehearsing, anticipating everything that was happening in the light of what was going to happen, stillbirth must be the archetypal human non-event. After all that, something must be registered as having happened, something must be thought or felt which is genuine and real, if the intense life of the last nine months is to be anything other than a complete write-off, a personal contribution to chaos.

Astrid Andersson Wretmark's study, *Perinatal Death* is focused upon the issue of reality confrontation, the necessity to, 'accept the child as a child, seeing it and planning for and attending the funeral service'. She looks closely into the growing number of rituals designed specifically for the death of children, reporting that in Great Britain and the USA, as well as in her native Scandinavia, 'The churches have been slow in catching up with the ritual needs which have been expressed by bereaved parents and by hospital staff' (1993, p.229). She is concerned with baptisms as well as funerals. The logic of this is inescapable: in order to say 'goodbye' properly, one must first have said 'hello', a fact of which the parents of stillborn children are painfully aware.

Baptising stillborn children presents more theological problems than does simply providing a funeral. According to Catholic teaching, 'sacraments are for the living, not the dead'. Wretmark examines some of the attempts made by Christian clergy, both Catholic and Protestant, to find a non-sacramental substitute for Holy Baptism. Notable among these is a Service of Baptismal Desire: 'Lord Jesus, we have followed your command and sought for baptism for this our dearly beloved child. ... In the mystery of your will, his/her life returns to you. May our desire that he/she should be a member of your body (the Church) be granted. May this candle symbolise your light in our saddened lives, and his/her incorporation into the body of your faithful people'(1993, p.227).[16]

This is an area of private and public life in which notable changes are at present taking place. Nowadays, people in Great Britain are more willing to talk about death without embarrassment than they were 40, or even 30 years ago. This is partly due to the number of books that have been written on the subject and the amount of research devoted to the human experience of grief and loss associated with it. Consequently those involved at the most personal level have been encouraged to talk about things which were not previously spoken of at all, except in private; and the willingness of people to reveal their feelings concerning the death of someone they loved, and the arrangements, or lack of them, for disposing of the body in a way which they would have found acceptable, has been a major factor in changing professional approaches to death. This is particularly true in the case of children. Writing about the death of her 36-hour-old daughter 30 years ago a mother reported that, 'Our desire to have a proper funeral and cremation was regarded as very odd by the funeral director and others. His comment, "We usually put them in someone else's coffin – why do you want to bother?", still bugs me enormously' (quoted in Walter 1990, p.273).

Tony Walter points to what he calls a revolution in social attitudes towards infant death which has been brought about by the determination of bereaved parents to treat even immature foetuses as people and accord them the dignity of a funeral. Gradually, more and more clergy have allied themselves with this aim: clergy who until recently refused Christian burial to even full-term babies that had not been baptised are now conducting funerals for foetuses of only 16 weeks. This change has been brought about by a much greater awareness of the emotional needs of bereaved people leading to an attitude of mind on the part of many clergy which pays more heed to pastoral concern than dogmatic orthodoxy. Recently, the Catholic Church in England and Wales has provided a liturgy for stillborn and miscarried children, and the Anglican Liturgical Commission has

16   The Rt Revd Peter Firth (1991) *The Hospital Chaplain*, September issue.

also looked in this direction. However, as Wretmark says: 'There is a dividing line between rituals which are created by those who have a close experience of dealing with loss and grief and those which are products of the writing-desk' (1993, p.273). The babies almost always die within a hospital setting, and it is largely hospital chaplains who have spearheaded this move. Andersson Wretmark draws attention to the fact that many of the unofficial rites used at these funerals have been created by parents in co-operation with hospital chaplains (1993, Chapters 12 and 13), men and women who have become aware through their personal involvement in the immediate situation of the extreme need at such a time and in such a place for the affirmation of meaning represented by the funeral.

In the area of memorialisation, however, modern Anglican clergy have not always been as supportive of mourners as their predecessors were. When it comes to providing some kind of lasting evidence that somebody has actually lived – for however short a time – and really died, the parents' requests to erect what they consider to be a suitable memorial have frequently been ruled out of court (this is actually a decision of professional lawyers retained by the Church) if their ideas do not conform to contemporary aesthetic standards. Where plain black stones are *de rigueur*, for example, white marble angels are unacceptable. In other places a strict control may be exercised over the wording on tombstones: familiar names and endearments are politely formalised or excluded altogether. These things are experienced as punitive by bereaved people, whatever the circumstances of their bereavement may be. In the case of those who have lost a beloved son or daughter they can be extremely harmful and cause people who are already psychologically threatened to become psychiatrically ill (Grainger 1992, p.2).

Churches, cemeteries and crematoria may lay down rules about memorialisation, but it is the instinctive reaction of the grief-stricken which leaves its mark on people's imagination. Perhaps the increasing amount of red tape and mystification surrounding memorialisation of the dead has contributed to the growing understanding that sincerity and spontaneity may stand instead of permanence, and that 'the best we can do' may be even more significant in some circumstances than the most elaborate and weighty tombstone. The tragic incident at Enniskillen in Northern Ireland on Remembrance Sunday, when members of the congregation at a war memorial service were murdered by the IRA, started a new tradition of do-it-yourself memorials, banks of flowers laid down at the actual scene of death. Somehow the frailty of this kind of memorial is its strength because it speaks so eloquently of that vulnerability which is the real power of love. The practice has spread rapidly since Enniskillen, so that it now takes in other times and places where death has occurred in tragic circumstances, particularly road accidents involving children. Here the memorials are not quite so temporary; when the flowers have died, the teddy bears and dolls remain, tied to the lamp-posts.

The year 1995 saw the foundation of The National Funerals College. This was an attempt to improve existing arrangements for death in Great Britain by working towards greater understanding and co-operation on the part of the various elements that make up the 'death industry' – funeral directors, superintendents of privately run and municipally owned cemeteries and crematoria, clergy and Church authorities, associations and individuals involved in counselling bereaved people, and anyone else who may consider that both the families of those who have died, and dead people themselves, deserve a better service than they are at present receiving. In the words of the College chairman, Malcolm Johnson:

> The average British funeral is a miserable and disappointing affair. For those who are not well-known figures or members of churches – most of us – the contemporary funeral lacks meaningful symbolism, dignity, adequate time and comfort for those who mourn. More particularly, it will pass without an informed and thoughtful appreciation of the life just ended. (Johnson 1996, Introduction)

Professor Johnson goes on to mention other typical features of the modern funeral: a 'contentless, diluted form of religious service' with 'a scratched-together and unsatisfactory account of the dead person'; crematorium arrangements which allow too short a time for serious remembrance, and which herd mourners into and through chapels on a production-line schedule – all of this arranged by a funeral director, 'who will have hired a minister, priest or other conductor of funerals to perform a minimal form of ritual that neither sustains nor properly farewells' (1996, Introduction).

These words of Professor Johnson reveal the real concern that the College has for the state of mind of mourners at an average British funeral. The Charter as a whole, however, goes further than this by paying regard to another aspect of funerals which may trouble and distress those who attend them. This is the question as to whether or not the funeral would have pleased or displeased the person most immediately concerned, the person whose funeral it actually is – is this what he or she would have wanted? What would he or she say about it? Would he or she be reassured or disgusted by what is being done and said on his or her behalf? In this regard, the Charter is anthropologically sensitive, concentrating upon the wishes and intentions of individuals concerning their own funerals. As unique human beings, they are brought back to the centre of our thinking about death so that the funeral can be an eloquent statement about a life that has been lived, rather than simply an effective kind of bereavement therapy –

which, of course, it can only be if it presents an authentic picture of a real person.[17]

The Shape of Death – The Motif of Reintegration in Funerals (The Post-Liminal Phase)

1. *The funeral itself*

   The funeral itself with its tripartite shape, which includes dismissal and disintegration (chaos), is the most important symbol of integration. The Roman Catholic order preserves this shape. In Protestant Europe and America it survives in a form which is severely hampered by being curtailed after the dismissal stage. The Protestant funeral has three stages, certainly: a 'service of the word', a 'commendation to God' and 'the committal of the body' either to be cremated or buried. These add up to a single pre-liminal ritual, which has to perform the overall integrating role originally carried out by the extended rite of passage. Memorial services, performed some time later, may be used to restore the original outline.

2. *Post-liminal ceremonies and time-limited mourning*

   a. *A succession of memorial services*, usually with one special memorial service each year; Japan (seven monthly services), Ashanti (five services.).

   b. *Three related services*: India (Hindu, Toda), Burma (Kachins).

3. *Cults of ancestor worship*

   a. *Annual feasts of the dead*: Rumania ('Ancestor's' Days), Russia ('Ancestors' Saturday' and 'Commemoration of the Dead'), Poland, Hungary, Spain, Austria, Brazil, Mexico, Ireland (All Saints' and All Souls'), Parsees (Farraden and Muktad).

   b. *Integration as a cultural institution*: Dahomey, Melanesia (Kiriwanians), Cuna Indians, Africa (among the Edo, the possession of a father who is

17   In an article which appeared in the *Guardian* on 8 February 1997, the year after she died, Jessica Mitford struck one final blow at the use of funerals for purposes of commercial exploitation. Her target in this case was the American funeral giant S.C.I: 'Its 1994 annual report to stock holders vibrates with pride: "Service Corporation International experienced the most dynamic year in its history in 1994, reaching new milestones in revenues and net incomes while establishing a solid presence in the European funeral industry." Revenues exceeded $1 billion as holdings grew to include 1,471 funeral homes, 220 cemeteries and 102 crematoriums. Its crowning achievement was the takeover of fifteen per cent of British funeral establishments.' Miss Mitford is dead (her own funeral cost $562.31, 'sea-scattering included'), but the National Funeral College fights on for the same cause.

a properly accredited ancestor of the tribe, as distinct from merely one of the *ighele-erinbhin*, or unincorporated ghosts, is a key factor in the fabrication of the new, re-formed, social order which follows the death of an important personage. A proper social balance must be maintained, and the dignity of having powerful or significant ghostly connections makes up for inferiority in other spheres), Catholic cultures (notably Mexico, where Catholic and native Indian beliefs are intertwined), China, Korea, Japan ('The souls of the dead are welcomed home and relatives and near neighbours make food offerings at the graves of the newly dead') (Habenstein and Lamers 1963, p.47).

4. *Ways of preserving the body*

This is carried out in many different ways, ranging from the embalming processes which are part of normal American and European practice, to actual mummification. In contrast, natives of Papua New Guinea make wooden images of the dead which they keep in their own homes.

5. *Graves, Mausolea, Ossuaries, Columbaria*

In some shape or form there is almost always a tangible memorial to the dead. Cemeteries throughout the world reproduce the architecture of the living in order to provide the dead with a symbolic lodging place. The tombs of Egypt, China and classical Europe were half temple, half monument; they have been reproduced in the graveyards of Europe and America by later generations as a way of underlining the dignity and timelessness of death. There are of course a very great number of cultural variations on this theme. In Persia, for example, chapels built upon graves are furnished with furniture and pictures and looked after by caretakers. South American Catholics construct elaborate mausolea as palaces for the dead (particularly Brazil and San Salvador). The Buganda of Uganda store the skulls of dead kings in temples. The Jivaro of the East Andes bury the dead in the houses they used to live in, and then build a new one for the living. Cuna Indian cemeteries are built to resemble native villages where the dead are buried in their hammocks. At the other end of the scale of permanence, huts are built by bereaved Ashanti and furnished with cooking pots, only to be taken down again the same night. In Christian countries, the churchyard or cemetery still serves as a way of reminding the living of those they have promised not to forget. Graves, tombs, mausolea, columbaria, are places traditionally regarded as sacramental for the dead. As C.S. Lewis says: 'A six-by-three foot flower bed has become Mum' (1961, pp.19, 20).

6. *Traditions symbolising fellowship with the dead*

Yugoslavia – the body exhumed, sprinkled with wine and re-buried;
Bali – water allowed to drip over the corpse on to rice, which is then
formed into an image of the dead person and eaten by the mourners;
Ashanti – the head man touches the coffin with two branches of a tree,
thereby separating the dead person's soul from his or her body – one
branch is kept to adorn the head man's sleeping place and the other is
buried with the corpse; Australian Warramunga – a widow stands
beneath the tree in which her dead husband has been buried in order to
'absorb his juices'; Ireland – clay pipes smoked at the funeral wake are
laid on the grave or kept besides the fireplace; Panama – a sprig of basil
is kept in a glass of water; Persia – when the burial is over, the
mourners retreat several paces from the grave and then return to it,
signifying that the dead person sees and recognises them; Turkey – a
light is kept burning in the dead person's room. Some of the dismissal
motifs mentioned at the end of Chapter 2 can be interpreted equally
well as symbols of reintegration. After all, an exit suggests an entrance
and may just as easily be used as one, if this is appropriate.

5

The Rite of Passage

All that I have been saying in the last chapter, both about the characteristic realism of funerals and their reality-promoting function, depends on certain aspects of the nature of corporate ritual itself. One aspect, as we have seen, is the *cathartic* effect of a ceremony in which the salient facts of human grieving are portrayed in the most vivid and dramatic form so that the actuality of loss is brought home in an intensified way to the bereaved, who find themselves forced to face up to what has happened to them. Descriptions of some of the funeral rituals of the world and the shattering effect that they have on bereaved people suggest a kind of psychological 'flooding', a technique employed by some clinical psychologists in which the emotionally traumatised are made to live through the process of adjustment to the presence of an unbearable reality in an intensified form and at a greatly accelerated rate in order to remove their initial distress as quickly as possible. This is a kind of desensitisation by emotional exhaustion, the rapid cauterisation of a wound which may otherwise, if it is allowed to go on bleeding, take a very much longer time to heal.[1]

---

1   Particularly interesting in this connection is the work done by Dr R.W. Ramsay at Amsterdam University. Dr Ramsay describes his approach to bereavement therapy as, 'a guided and systematic form of abreaction carried to the point where the negative emotions are extinguished ... there are similarities with Gestalt therapy, psycho-drama, rational emotive therapy and implosive emotional therapy ... The function of the therapist is to confront the client repeatedly with the fact of loss and all that it entails, to break down the denial, to evoke the depression, guilt, anxieties and aggressions until these emotions are extinguished and there is no further reaction to loss. This is usually done in lengthy sessions of enforced confrontation (usually 2 hours) with no possibility of escape. Various items which can be expected to evoke a reaction are presented in imagination until one hits home and the client reacts. The therapist then allows the reaction, be it a crying fit or an aggressive outburst, to take its course and subside. The therapist then presents that item again and again, until no further reaction occurs. For example, with a woman who has lost her husband, an item such as physical contact can be worked through in a hierarchical manner, from never again being able to hold his hand, through never being able to kiss him again, to never again feeling him stroking her breasts... The therapist has to bear in mind constantly that he must work through all gradations, as well as the various components, of the grief process ... he keeps doggedly at it until the person is "burned out"'. Dr Ramsay points out that although he

Another aspect, perhaps a more basic one, is to be found in the *relational* identity of corporate ritual. Historians of religion such as Mercea Eliade maintain that the rite really functions in order to demonstrate a religious truth by means of the iconography of social interaction. In and through the rite, individual experience is treated in a social way, one which emphasises the individual's solidarity with the community and its ideals. Specifically, its action is one of 'homologisation', the identification of men and women with a sacred truth which is believed to hold society together by having a common reference to all human experience, whether individual or corporate. In this way, the rite mediates between man and his environment, making spiritual sense of all sorts of puzzling occurrences and irreconcilable facts. As we have seen, this is the same point that was made by anthropologists such as Malinowski, Turner and Geertz. Eliade (1957, 1958a and b) and Bouyer (1963), however, go further. In its primary, archetypal form, ritual is a sharing of persons in a cosmic event which involves no less than the renewal of nature by the re-creation of the world. Rituals take place in a 'sacred time', the symbolic re-presentation of the primal epoch of the world's beginning. As Marcel Mauss expresses it, 'festivals take place in Eternity' (Hubert and Mauss 1909, p.190f). They are concerned with Being-Itself, the root and ground of individual being, and set out to transcend existential divisions and limitations. Corporate rituals, it is maintained, afford us a glimpse of the ideal in the midst of the ordinary, an actual experience of 'heaven and earth'.

They do not say how such a thing can be, except insofar as to point out that the rite uses religious symbolism in order to communicate a divine reality to men and women. Perhaps we might take a closer look at what is involved. In the rite we are encouraged to regard human existence as a coming-together of separate selves, and human perfection as the perfection of love between persons. The people in the rite remain separate. They do not simply merge into one another, losing their identities. They are not engaged in conquest and evasion, but are spent in reciprocal giving and receiving, in *being in respect of* one another. Thus the rite is a demonstration of Charles William's dictum that 'perfection lies everywhere in interchange' (1937, p.248). In the rite this perfection is presented symbolically, because the rite is a work of art, and its value is a contingent value, or a value

uses, 'the psycho-analytic background of description about components of bereavement' and the notions of repression and denial of grief, his therapeutic attack has little resemblance to the dynamic approach. 'Talking about the situation is not the same thing as experiencing the emotions connected with the event... It is exactly those clients who failed to work it out verbally with family, friends, and others who are candidates for this form of therapy.' It should perhaps be pointed out that the therapist himself suffers a high degree of pain through having to cause pain to another person in a therapeutic relationship. 'This induction of pain and the frustration of not being allowed to ease it makes the carrying out of such therapy extremely unpleasant – probably as unpleasant as doctors found operations before anaesthetics were invented' (Ramsay Happee 1977, pp.53–64).

governed by contingency, by the human ability to create or evolve meaningful images.

Governed, but not compromised; for it is this contrived nature of the artistic symbol that gives it its authenticity, its value as an expression of human truthfulness. Man lives in the space between this symbolised perfection and his own contingent actuality. He cannot attain the wholeness whose image he casts within the special circumstances of the rite, for the rite is an empirically contrived world, an existence which he has drastically limited in scope in order to achieve the intense concentration of experience necessary for the act of focusing. By focusing the world he distorts it in order to see beyond it. The rite is an artefact, worlds away from the truth it depicts. And yet, because of this distance between actuality and aspiration – because of it and not in spite of it – our involvement with the ideal world to which we reach out is more wholehearted than ever, as, in our effort to leap the gap, we move away from ourselves towards the other. The ritual symbol itself is the human perfection of all meeting; it is distance that makes it so, for it is distance which allows relationship. There is no question of any kind of reduction of ideality by human limitation, only of a relation of otherness in which the self reaches out to what is not itself and in doing so discovers its own real identity in acknowledging its boundaries.

The moment of meeting is a timeless moment, allowing the rite to be a place of opportunity, a true point of departure. What seems to be a total dichotomy, a simple confrontation of the ideal and the actual, life as it should be and life as it is, is revealed as a mystery of potential unity. In the rite, whether their gestures and movements are solemn or light-hearted, men and women move among one another to transcend themselves. In the ritual dance, they establish their willingness and ability to live towards one another in the relationship of love. They do this not by losing themselves in a wave of generalised emotion, surrendering to the collective idealism of the group, but by celebrating the conditions involved in, and dictated by, their own individual personhood. For the rite is a demonstration of the ability to achieve true mutuality, the mutuality which is an interchange of separatenesses, and emerges not from any kind of confusion of identities, but from the free exchange of individuality by people who are essentially autonomous yet can only discover their autonomy in the art of bestowing it on another; who only *live* in relation to one another. What is true of the intricate organisation of the ritual dance is true of all rituals, even the simplest and most sober ones, insofar as they represent the purposive celebration of relationship used as a message about the truth of existence.

Thus the rite reveals itself as a microcosm of the human condition, and establishes the validity of Gabriel Marcel's (1965) claim that the human body is the symbol of man's freedom and not simply the main piece of evidence about his finitude. It is an acted parable of the interrelation of man and man which the ambiguous identity of the human body – at once the limiter and the liberator of the human spirit – expands into a living symbol of the relation of the conditioned and the unconditioned, of selfishness and love. In the interplay of self and other acted out in ritual, the relation between man and God is symbolised.

In these ways the horizontal movement becomes a vertical one. The rite becomes the authentic vehicle of idealistic aspiration, of *religious* aspiration, portrayed in countless rites of passage which, in a scenario of departure, journeying and arrival, symbolise the active searching for a transcendent purpose and meaning whose presence is experienced in the action of the rite itself. Words must be found for this archaic movement of ontological aspiration, so that gesture may become concept, a translatable experience. For obvious cultural reasons which concern the handing on of vital human understanding, the language of gesture, of the pre-rational celebration of relational truths, must receive propositional form. In fact any number of mythological 'explanations' may accompany the fundamental, invariable. ritual progression. But the rite itself, in its typical form and at its basic level, does not change, however much its *dramatis personae* may vary from culture to culture and occasion to occasion. Quite simply, it moves from 'before' to 'after', in an ascending direction. It progresses from lower to higher, marking out man's desire for more perfect being. As Clem Gorman puts it in his book *Book of Ceremony,* 'ceremony always leads to higher ground' (1972, p.45). As we have seen in the preceding chapters, it makes its progression in three stages, and the decisive quality of its determination to make its distinctive gesture of aspiration is reinforced by the three-fold form it invariably assumes, in accordance with the basic model of change itself. It is the best way of all of giving form to intention, of shaping an expressive wish, of power-fully and explicitly proclaiming the attitude of mind of those who take part. Ritual leaves no doubt in the mind of either the participant or the spectator. It transforms uncertainty and ambiguity into a definite statement: 'We are the ones who feel this – who intend this – who believe this'. Others may not have been aware of these things before; indeed, from time to time, those who are involved themselves may have forgotten them. But now we know. *We all know.*

Ritual changes things by establishing them. It conquers uncertainty and puts an end to states of flux. I said earlier that there is evidence to show that healthy mental activity works towards the elaboration of creative patterns. Funerals have an aesthetic effect, for the shattering of life-patterns by the death of a loved person is here not simply negated. It is used for the purpose of achieving a greater wholeness, a more significant affirmation of value. The ideas in which this life-out-of-death event clothes itself are the ideas of myth, the unknown personal given definite form, the elusive and beckoning meeting of otherness; the language in which it is expressed is the language of the rite and of corporate ceremony. This is the precise way in which the funeral 'takes death into itself'. In its mythical scenario, whether this is portrayed explicitly or symbolised in the actions of commendation and committal, a complete and perfectly articulated event is envisaged, moving from life through death into life again – not the static concept of life, but the ongoing reality of *being alive*. The life of both the dead and the living will be renewed as an ongoing corporate experience. The significance of the past will help the future not merely to take place, but to grow in value, in depth and quality of experience. In religious language, fellowship with the blessed dead, those who have arrived at their journey's end and have profited by the experience, will reinforce the experience of their survivors, making it more rich, more full, more real. To do this it establishes the point of death, accepting it as the necessary preface to an onward movement into life.

The progression is from a known reality to one that is not yet known, and so on. Here the 'known reality' is death; death as the personal experience of suffering bereavement; death as the actual presence of a corpse. The funeral's two primary purposes are, first of all, to establish this reality by means of a dramatic presentation of the facts, and, second, having brought home the real nature of the event itself, to use the interplay of person and person within the rite to express the truth about human relationship recognised as a *religious* truth, one which is at once ultimate and open-ended, the goal of human searching and the mode in which that search must be carried on.

These two purposes are in fact the same. The funeral makes an a-personal, or even anti-personal, happening into a human event, in accordance with the action of the rite itself, which is a form-bestowing mechanism, something which makes happenings into events. The funeral is a demonstration of the truth that growth depends on definition; 'meanings require endings'. The relational event contributes its own innate power to the attainment of clarity of experiences by the establishment of an existential landmark, a signpost for the future. 'This, and this precisely, this and nothing else, is what has happened. This consequently is where you must start from.'

It is the religious power of the rite, in the sense of its inalienable relational significance, that establishes the event of death in the mind of the bereaved person; and it does so by setting its seal on the past in order that the future may be allowed to take place. Only the rite, as the demonstration of an ideal way of being to which we may aspire, and in which, through our love for one another, we are already sharing, can do such a thing. The sacramental identity of ritual underlines and transfigures the brusque instrumentality of its immediate effect, according to which it acts as a period set at the end of the story of a life, concerned solely to establish an ending and permit the possibility of a new beginning. For in this symbolism of sharing the rite proclaims the authentically religious message that life is to be discovered not in contrast to, but actually within the event of death itself. In the rite, more than anywhere else, 'the medium is the message'. The message of the funeral rite is particularly clear. We escort a dead person upon the first stage of his journey; we 'go with him to the riverside', thereby proclaiming in the action itself a common humanity, a common willingness to suffer on behalf of others and to share in the grief of the bereaved; a common vulnerability to the inherent dangers of living and dying, the sudden thrombosis and the slowly hardening artery, the powder-keg circumstances of our common mortality. We go out of fellow-feeling, out of sympathy for the grief-stricken, to give them the assurance of our emotional support.

We go for less tangible reasons, too. These are to do with a common basic human dignity that cannot, must not, be removed, and demands acknowledgment of its birthright. It is this that makes the most unassuming occasion an affirmation of value, a worthwhile celebration of humanness. Here in small, unspectacular funerals, the burial of neglected people, rather than on great state occasions or at the obsequies of the popular and beloved, is the true significance of the rite revealed. When somebody dies whose relatives cannot be traced and a few neighbours turn out to say goodbye to the old fellow whom they had never really liked very much anyway; when the number of patients in the female psycho-geriatric ward at the mental hospital is reduced by the death of one isolated old woman, and the sister in charge brings along half-a-dozen patients, all equally old, equally isolated, to pay their last respects 'because she hasn't anybody, you know'; these are the times when the funeral really counts, because this is what funerals are really about. There is nothing merely sentimental in making this claim. It is intended to be taken quite literally. Such unpropitious occasions proclaim the real function of the funeral in the clearest and least ambiguous way. They are not prompted by considerations of social prestige, or by the desire to make a show and impress the neighbours or reinforce the existing hierarchical structure within a community. They are not ways of assuaging the guilt of ambivalence, in accordance with one of the most common and plausible psychological rationales of funeral display; indeed, these archetypal, critical, front-line funerals are noted for their absence of display. They are not particularly valuable as outlets for powerful feelings of grief on the part of the bereaved, because there is often no one present who comes into the category of a bereaved person. On these occasions it is neither an individual nor a community that is bereaved, but humanity. When the unpopular, isolated, socially stigmatised person dies and is buried with due ceremony, then Donne's famous sermon is revealed as simple, existential fact rather than superb rhetoric: 'Any man's death diminishes me because I am involved in mankind. And therefore, never send to know for whom the bell tolls: it tolls for Thee'.

The assertion of human worth, the honour due to human dignity, only demands a quorum because it is a symbolic statement, and symbolism functions according to paradox and not rational assessment. The less likelihood there is of anyone turning out to say goodbye, the more valuable is the action of the few who do; the more they represent mankind as a whole and express reality, the true state of affairs, for mankind. The same is true, of course, for the bereaved person who attends the funeral of someone whom he has greatly loved, making himself go, often against the advice of his family and friends who are as frightened as he is that he will not be able to bear it. Such people are aware of a greater priority than that of keeping calm and avoiding pain: the instinctive compulsion to assert the dignity and importance of persons. Where personality and individuality are seen to be in danger in institutions for the control of large numbers of sick or homeless people, or under war-time emergency conditions when the dead must be buried in the presence of the enemy themselves, the necessity to say something about human worth is at its greatest. The action of burial or cremation, the religious action of disposal, says all that can be said. When this action involves considerable danger to the people performing it, the men who must crawl through acres of mud in a hail of shells or hack away at the stones and rubble, working waist-deep in a flooded mine-shaft to retrieve the bodies, it speaks louder and more forcibly than any argument, says more for faith in the essential meaning and value of life than any sermon.[2]

There is a value that transcends time without denying it, which asserts the present reality of human events yet allows them final significance. Its symbolic embodiment in funeral rites brings home the factual nature of death by asserting the importance of life. The funeral is the celebration of a lived life, a completed gesture, an achieved value. It takes all the gestures and movements of the past and projects them into a final statement, a statement about finality in which it

---

2   'Pledged to recover the bodies of comrades who died in bitter fighting ... two battalions of U.S. Marines pushed forward slowly today against stubborn North Vietnamese resistance ... "We don't leave our people", said First Lieut. Jerry Howell of Almedo, California. "I'm sure they'd do the same for me"' (*New York Times*, 4 July 1967). The American attitude seems more remarkable than the attitude of Homer's Greeks and Trojans because of the secular nature of the age in which we are living. In 1975, the Japanese and American authorities co-operated in the attempt to retrieve the bodies of the 86 crew members of the Japanese submarine I-169 sunk in World War II and discovered by chance 30 years later by a diving expedition. Nearer home, in 1973 30 teams of rescue workers worked for a total of 130 hours at Lofthouse Colliery in the West Riding of Yorkshire to recover the bodies of seven miners trapped there. The work went on for nearly a month, long after any real hope of getting the men out alive had vanished. (A Home Office pathologist is reported as having said that they were almost certainly killed in the first rush of water.) In the event, only one body was recovered; but no-one grudged the time and effort spent in the unsuccessful battle to recover the other six bodies. 'If they were my men,' said the coroner, 'I'd want them out.' Another striking example was reported in *The Times* on 11 November 1996: 'After the wreckage of a Battle of Britain fighter plane was found beneath the pavement of a seaside town with human remains inside, a grieving relative of the young pilot said yesterday she could not rest until his grave was dug up to reveal whether it contains his remains: "If it turns out that his body is not in the grave but is in the aeroplane we will want a second funeral, with full military honours".'

somehow manages to find hope. In itself the assertion of value is an encouragement. Its public proclamation has a healing effect upon the wound of grief. The testimony of the bereaved people who have taken part in funeral services supports this claim. It is possible for a funeral to relieve a previously in supportable burden of grief in a way which transcends any kind of simplistic explanations about 'getting things off one's chest'. The funeral is much more the symbolic embodiment of an idea than a kind of institutionalised expression of an emotional process. A bereaved person will have to 'work through' the stages or components of grieving after the funeral service. The authenticity of the expression of grief at funerals is of no direct consequence – which is why familiar criticisms of funeral traditions which make use of hired mourners falls wide of the mark. The main purpose of a funeral is to signify the event of a death. The reality of death, both the actual death of the person who has died and the reactive trauma of the people who are bereaved, is symbolised in a ritual enactment which aims at its own kind of completeness. In the funeral, death and its concomitant states of *mind* (for the bereaved) and of *being* (for the dead person) are symbolised, not reproduced. The relationship between the funeral and the work of grieving is one of contiguity rather than congruity; the funeral's purpose is to institute the work of grieving not to contain it or complete it. Its comprehensiveness in its most typical form is the comprehensiveness that all funeral rituals aspire to (even the minimal services to which we are reduced by the spirit of the age and the schedules of crematoria) – a symbolic comprehensiveness, the basic and irreducible iconography of essential change, which must first of all be asserted ideationally before it can be ratified existentially.

The funeral is concerned with the event of death. Its therapeutic effect is to allow therapy to take place. It is not in itself a form of treatment for states of 'pathological grieving'. It would, of course, be very difficult to gauge the therapeutic effect of funeral attendance upon the bereaved by trying to produce scientific evidence to demonstrate that a person suffering from protracted or pathological grief might have avoided this reaction if he had only attended the funeral; it would be even harder, if not downright impossible, to predict the onset of pathological grieving in the case of a survivor who was unwilling or unable to follow the coffin to the grave.

On the other hand, there is considerable evidence that refusal to acknowledge the event of death can have serious effects of a medical nature. There is reasonable agreement in the medical literature that sooner or later the death of a loved person must be acknowledged not only in theory but in fact, as something that has to be lived. The purpose of the process of grieving is to incorporate the fact of bereavement within the ongoing living awareness of the bereaved person. Grief work is no mere optional employment, undertaken by the sentimental (or emotionally inclined). It is necessary to the survival of the individual as a whole person. The grief work must be done. The promised debt, the price of human loving, has to be paid. We might even add that the grief work *will* be done. Sooner or later, correctly or incorrectly, completely or incompletely, straightforwardly or in convoluted ways, *it will be done*. It may be, as Murray Parkes claims, that the processes of post-traumatic denial are psychologically necessary as well as inevitable because the impact of loss is too great to be borne without serious and perhaps permanent damage to the delicate adjustment of an individual's 'coping mechanisms'. But denial must be no more than a stage on the journey through acknowledgment to integration and adjustment. Even more effectively and dramatically than the thought of our own death, the death of someone who has become a part of the substance of our life 'gives us pause', halts us in our tracks, causes us to hold back in a desperate instinctive effort to cling to what has only just stopped being the case, the state of affairs that existed the moment before last. For the sake of life, for the sake of the future, things must find a new way of being, a new normality. Time must be resumed. The clock must be restarted, the interrupted meal cleared away, the starkly superfluous chair put back in the corner so that, when the time comes, it can be drawn up again to the fire. For the sake of the future, the past must be recognised. As T.S. Eliot wrote, the future can be built only upon the real past.[3]

Thankfully, most people survive the period of grieving at their own rate and in their own way, without the need for a doctor. That is, they do not become ill as a result of their experience. Some, however, do not even start on the journey, particularly if the shock of bereavement has been too sudden and the habit of association, of a shared life and a common experience, is too securely entrenched. If for example, a husband suddenly dies after half a century of married life, his widow will go on setting his place at the table, hold long conversations with his empty chair, tell others of the plans they have been making together. This kind of total denial can be almost impregnable; it is, doctors tell us, untreatable. Indeed, there is no need to interfere with it, because the surviving partner has found his or her own way of preserving a kind of balance. It is where denial is only partial and a sense of reality persists in intruding itself that clinical reactions, usually in the form of reactive depression or phobic states, tend to show themselves.

A good deal of work has been done to try and find out what causes pathological bereavement of this kind. Murray Parkes and his associates (1972) have carried out several investigations with groups of bereaved people with the

---

3   In 'The Family Reunion' written in 1939. The universal tendency towards psychological denial of loss has been remarked on by many doctors and psychologists, especially Lindemann (1944): 'One of the big obstacles to this work seems to be the fact that many patients try to avoid the intense distress connected with the grief experience and to avoid the expressions of emotion necessary for it' (p.141). For cultural expressions of psychological denial, see Gorer (1965), Mitford (1963), Hinton (1967), and so on.

aim of finding out exactly what kind of bereavement reaction could reasonably be considered 'normal' so that they could proceed to distinguish the specific factors involved in the aetiology of abnormal grief. In the USA a group of psychiatrists working at the Harvard Medical School studied the post-bereavement experiences of a sample of 68 widows and widowers under the age of 45, who were 'interviewed fourteen months after bereavement and compared with a control group of sixty-eight married men and women of the same age, sex, occupational class and family size'. The first group showed evidence of 'depression and general emotional disturbance as reflected in restlessness and insomnia' (Parkes 1972, p.21); their intake of tobacco, alcohol and tranquilisers had increased since bereavement, and there was also a tendency for them to complain of physical symptoms (Parkes 1972, p.21).[4]

The most interesting results, however, concerned the predictive value of the investigation, particularly as regards the presence of powerful negative feelings on the part of the bereaved. 'The principal conclusions to be drawn from this study,' says Dr Parkes, 'are that intense grief, anger or self-reproach expressed shortly after bereavement, particularly if it is not declining in intensity within six weeks, predicts poor outcome a year later' (1972, p.214). There seems little doubt that emotions which the survivor finds psychologically threatening – feelings of resentment towards the dead person because of his past behaviour, or anger because of his action in dying and depriving his widow of his companionship and support – are a source of guilt which acts against the ventilation of grief in the bereaved and so hinders the work of reintegration and the restoration of psychological balance. Parkes's investigation into the incidence of emotional ambivalence among bereaved psychiatric patients provides evidence that such feelings contribute very noticeably to post-bereavement breakdown (1964, 1965). On the other hand, anything that tends to inhibit the spontaneous expression of feeling immediately after bereavement (and this is often the effect of the presence of unacceptable feelings of anger, resentment or guilt) has been shown to protract the overall period of mourning considerably. The 25 London widows in Parkes's 1972 study showed a tendency towards chronic grieving which increased in violence as the weeks passed, in inverse ratio to the absence of powerful feeling on the occasion of the death itself. In these cases, the end of three months revealed a worse state of affairs than had existed at the beginning for the widows whose initial grief reaction had been dramatic and profound.

4   A four year longitudinal study carried out between 1990 and 1996 by the School of Health and Community Studies at De Montfort University, Leicester, shows that men who had recently been widowed had declined noticably in mental health, morale and social functioning (Bennett 1997).

The evidence seems to show, then, that bereaved people need to be encouraged to grieve, and that inhibition of feeling, although it may be an automatic reaction in the initial stages of bereavement, should not be encouraged to continue. If it does continue this suggests the presence of attitudes and emotions which the bereaved person feels must be kept hidden. The psychological 'deadening' which follows trauma is in these cases reinforced by the processes of repression; the sense of something wrong, something incomplete, an unsatisfactory relationship, a record not yet set straight, the haunting awareness of 'unfinished business', is very strong.[5]

The aim of all therapy concerned with bereaved people is the achievement of a state of mind of restored personal and social wholeness. This has been described in various ways: Dr Ramsay (1975) calls it 'reintegration'; Dr Hobson (1970) 'reincorporation'; Geoffrey Gorer (1965) talks of 're-established physical homeostasis ... interest again directed outwards'; Murray Parkes (1972), of 'gaining new identity'; Dr Hinton (1967), of 'reinstitution'; Dr Bowlby (1960), simply of 'hope'. The bereaved person emerges from his experience saddened but optimistic, as one who has completed an arduous journey. He has not come through unscathed, and he will almost certainly have lost any excess baggage he may have been carrying on the way. Only if the journey has proved too difficult and the way too long will he have needed the help of doctors or psychologists, although all along he will have needed the support of friends. The process by which a bereaved person frees himself from the crippling aspects of grief is very much one of re-emergence; re-emergence into clarity of mind, out of the shadowy valley into the sunlight. As Peter Marris has said, the process of grieving itself is aimed at making a meaningless experience intelligible by finding ways to re-interpret it (1958). C.S. Lewis (1961), describing his own bereavement, speaks in terms of the gradual recovery of a true mental image of his wife.

Truth, clarity, honesty, candour. These are the things which are lost when we suffer the death of someone whom we dearly love. The situation arouses such strong negative emotions that the person involved tries to avoid thinking about it. It is not that we intend to deceive either ourselves or other people, not at least after the first instinctive reaction. Instead we lose our ability to identify truth, to locate reality, to distinguish it from despair and depression on the one hand and wish-fulfilment on the other. It is this confusion which gets in our way when we try to take stock of what has happened to us. It is not our separation from the dead that prevents our finding them again, but confusion and fear – the confusion which is the long-term result of profound existential trauma, the fear that the

5   Elizabeth Kubler-Ross (1970) describes a similar situation with regard to people who are prevented or hindered in coming to terms with their approaching death by others who cannot accept their own feelings on the subject.

confusion will never cease and we shall never again see clearly. It is confusion which is the enemy of truth and clarity, and consequently of *acceptance*.

The practice of organised mourning is a powerful agent in clearing away confusion. 'It insists that the death has occurred, repeatedly demonstrating this fact in various ways over a few days, so that the bereaved, whatever their state of mind, accept the painful knowledge, assimilate it and begin to plan accordingly' (Hinton 1967, p.184). John Hinton goes on to repeat what others have said about the value of traditional funeral practices in establishing reality: 'Viewing the body and taking part in the funeral emphasize beyond all doubt that the person is really dead. The condolences, the discussion of the deceased in the past tense, the newspaper announcements, the public recognition of the dead, all affirm the loss' (1967, p.184). The funeral above all establishes and proclaims the event of death. The clear outline of the rite, the unequivocal gesture of the human body, its solemn and precise pronouncement of an action completed, a life achieved, is the most authoritative voice of all. Even more than the grave monument, the funeral says clearly and finally, 'It is finished. Here he lies. Make no mistake; he is dead'.

It seems strange to us that such a communication should permit the emergence of hope. Yet that is precisely what it does do. The acceptance of the fact of death permits the restoration of relationship with the dead. For relationship is not confusion but separation, even as love is the confirmation of another's identity. To love is to recognise the particular uniqueness of another person; to value another's self-hood. We love the other because they are, for us, still uniquely other. When we visualise them in the mind's eye they detach themselves from everything and everyone else, which is why the mental picture of someone whom we deeply love has a kind of 'halo effect' around it. In fact we love them for this, for having evaded us. Although they are central to our world, we have never really managed to incorporate them in that world. We can locate them, but we cannot subdue them.

For when we really love, we relinquish all our rights over another, and not least of these is the human impulse to categorise, to reduce a presence to an experience. This is not a right but an inevitable process, a 'mental mechanism', part of simply being human. We look, we take, we include: we cannot help it and are surely not to be blamed for it. And yet, in love, we surrender even this. We look and we stay. In love, we abide in the moment of meeting. Love is not a mechanism but a mystery; not a transaction but a consummation, a truly miraculous happening.

All the same, this miracle makes use of mechanisms, even as spirit emerges dialectically from structures. Anything which runs counter to our existential tendency towards self-aggrandisement at others' expense, any way of behaving whose action and result expresses freedom and self-giving, is available to love; available for men and women to use for loving purposes, in the service of loving intention. The most potent and appropriate tool is art, which is the symbol of loving *interaction*. Art suggests and does not impose. It beckons, but does not, cannot, compel. By its very nature, it has foresworn compulsion – physical, intellectual or emotional. Even at its most violently expressive, art communicates gently; we are not forced to accept it. The funeral rite is man's resolution of death into the form of art.

This is not done in order to reduce the reality of death, but to transform the nature of that reality, to make it into a personal event instead of an impersonal, negative, meaningless interruption. The funeral does not answer the question posed by death, the final question of final meaning, because this is beyond the power of any human construct, however skilfully contrived. It only directs our attention in the right direction, to the place where answers to such questions are to be found, and leaves us free to discover whether or not we can find our answer there. The language of religious ritual is the language of art. The rite communicates with us in the way in which a work of art communicates: that is, by inviting a specific kind of question to which it provides its own kind of answer. The questions and answers of art are about relationship. Specifically, they are about the relationship between experience and aspiration, the world as everyday reality and the world as ideal truth, for art itself is the language of aspiration, of the sensibility of otherness, which reaches out towards what is not itself. But the suggestion implicit in art is that this ideal truth is itself personal, that its human reality is interpersonal, that its practical truth is the truth of between-ness. This is why a true work of art has no independent perfection, but welcomes us into relationship with the perfection that inspires it.

However, it may quite reasonably be objected that when I have said all this I have done no more than repeat the claim made by religiously inclined people from time immemorial: that certain ritual actions are religiously effective, that they mediate between worlds, that they provide a channel of communication between man and God which is available for the use of men, all things being of course 'available' for God's use. I am not trying to commend a theological doctrine about sacramental presence (although I believe such a doctrine to be true). I am talking about the value of relationship, which value is evident to most people whether they are 'religious' or not. Our attempts to restrain the dead, to demonstrate our love of them to ourselves and others by clinging to them, are wholly ill-advised. Our stubborn determination to *think* them into re-existence shows how little we understand about the dynamics of loving. We associate loving with having, when we should know that it is really about being; at least, it is about having in order to give away. As long as our energies are directed towards possession and away from relationship, our attempts to live in the presence of the departed can be nothing more than psychological tricks, an example of the 'sleight of mind' at which human beings seem particularly adept. It is inevitable that the shock of deprivation should have this effect on us – that we should seize hold of any source of comfort that comes to hand, whether this involves an inauthentic experience of the dead person's return or the equally inauthentic denial that he or she has ever actually departed. It is certainly 'normal' enough for us to deceive ourselves like this, to begin with at least. In the long run, though, it is a distortion and a disservice. The dead person was never like that. I cannot take him into myself this way, reducing him to an aspect of my own personality, a function of my own way of looking at the world. He was himself. If I loved him, then I serve him best by letting him be.

In this way the dead preserve their reality in our lives. By leaving them free to depart we encourage them to stay with us. For you can only have a relationship with someone when you know who they are and are willing to allow them to know it too. The rite asserts the existential importance of another person. In this case, it has much to say about the personal value of the man or woman who has died, his or her worth as an individual.

In the same way, you can only have a relationship with someone when you know *where* they are. This is very important. The fact that they may be a good way off, either in place or time, so that it is physically impossible to contact them, does not affect the truth of this statement at all. We have already recognised the notational effect of the funeral, its function as an existential landmark. The funeral, we have said, locates a person's death as an event in time. In religious thought it is an event which is given a very definite spatial reference; at this point a new and crucial stage in a vital progression is attained, and no amount of 'demythologisation' can detract from the awareness which the symbol is intended to induce. The time between a man's life and his death inevitably suggests a kind of journey; this is very generally agreed, however much disagreement there may be about what happens to him after he has died. A man has either finished his journey at this stage or he has passed beyond it. But something definite has happened, something recognisable, something that can be thought about. He has been *located*. He may be somewhere else, but he is at least somewhere. Either in eternity or time – for the past is a place, too.

Candour, realism, honesty. Identification and location, knowing who a person is and where he is. In all its varied cultural guises, this is the symbolism of the funeral and this is its enabling power. It divides the living from the dead, and in dividing them pronounces the terms of their reunion. This, it says, is what has happened; this and nothing else. It is this separateness, this distinction, this line firmly drawn between life and death that summons us into the truth of the happening, attracted by what Martin Buber (1957, p.67) calls a 'polar unity'. We find ourselves inescapably summoned into the reality of our situation as we reach out across the abyss towards the beckoning other; united, like Ovid's Pyramus and Thisbe, by the very obstacle that divides us. Thus in presenting us with death the rite teaches us about life; in confirming our despair it allows our hope. It is a y, its supporters advocate a new flexibility of approach in which more care is given to taking account of the unique family context of the person who has died, so that the occasion will be much less awkward, from a social point of view, than the standard British funeral. In Peter Jupp's phrase, funerals show signs of being 'more personal, more prepared, more positive' (1997). From the point of view of social symbolism, funerals are becoming more expressive of individual family values and meanings, and consequently better able to speak to twentieth century society at both individual and institutional levels. (This applies even to large scale public occasions: I am writing this less than a week after the funeral of Diana, Princess of Wales.) The 'do-it-yourself' funeral movement, for example, claims to be 'interested in the 300- and 400-year-old tradition where the funeral was (really) a family event' (Steve Nutt, *The Daily Telegraph*, 26 June, 1997), genuinely expressing the life experience of an unique cluster of personal relationships.

Acting the story, giving it the special force of a living memorial, requires an understanding of the ways in which corporate ritual functions. Welfare State, a theatre company based at present in the English Lake District, has specialised for more than 30 years in the construction of passage rites which are unique social and personal events. Nowadays it concentrates increasingly on funerals, reflecting a growing awareness within the community at large of the part played by corporate ritual in helping people find their own kinds of sense in situations where corporate and individual morale are severely challenged (Fox and Gill 1997). The kind of ritual adventure offered by Welfare State has, for many people and situations, only a limited appeal. The movement to restore the three-fold ritual shape to funerals, so that their ability to act as symbols of change and channels of spiritual growth may be understood and appreciated, continues to make progress in ways that are less revolutionary. For example, in one such experiment, described recently in the *Church Times*, cremation was timed to take place in the morning, to be followed in the afternoon by a service in church, and a final ceremony for the interment of ashes. In this way it was found possible to preserve the underlying ritual movement from dismissal to reintegration, encouraging the mourners to express their awareness of loss in the protected 'in-between' space of the church service (M.C. Stanton-Saringer, *Church Times*, 13 June, 1997). Even under such circumstances, the three-fold rite continues to bring us comfort and hope.

References

Abraham, K. (1988) *Selected Papers in Psychoanalysis.* (Originally published 1927), London: Maresfield.

Acquinas, St. T. (1988) *Summa Theologiae.* London: Sheed and Ward.

Alexander, I.E. and Adlerstein, A.M. (1958) 'Studies in the psychology of death.' *Journal of Genetic Psychology 93,* 167-177.

Anouilh, J. (1954) *Antigone.* London: Harrap.

Anthony, S. (1940) *The Child's Discovery of Death.* London: RKP.

Avonson, E and Mills, J. (1953) 'Effect of severity of initiation on liking for a group', in D. Cartwright and A. Zander, (al) *Group Dynamics, Research and Theory,* q.v. 119-124.

Banton, M. (ed) (1966) *Anthropological Approaches to the Study of Religion.* London: Tavistock.

Bendann, E. (1930) *Death Customs.* London: Kegan Paul.

Bennett, K. (1997) Unpublished paper read at the Third International Conference on the Social Context of Death and Dying, Cardiff 1997.

Berger, P. (1973) *The Social Reality of Religion.* Harmondsworth: Penguin.

Bouyer, L. (1963) *Rite and Man,* London: Burns and Oates.

Bowlby, J. (1960) 'Grief and mourning in infancy and early childhood.' *The Psychoanalytic Study of the Child 15:* 9-52.

Bowlby, J. (1961) 'The process of mourning.' *Int. J. Psycho. Anal 44.* 317–40.

Bradbury, R.E. (1966) 'Fathers, elders and ghosts' in edo religion' in M. Banton (ed.) q.v. 127–153.

Brown, F. (1961) 'Depression and childhood bereavement.' *Journal of Mental Science 107,* 754–777.

Buber, M. (1957) *Pointing the Way.* London: Routledge & Kegan Paul.

Buber, M. (1966) *I and Thou.* Edinburgh: T. & T. Clark.

Camus, A. (1955) *The Myth of Sisyphus.* London: H. Hamilton.

Caplan, G. (1964) *Principles of Preventative Psychiatry.* London: Tavistock.

Cartwright, P. and Zander, A. (eds) (1953) *Group Dynamics, Research and Theory.* London: Tavistock.

Cope, G. (ed) (1970) *Dying, Death and Disposal.* London: SPCK.

Davies, J.G. (1972) *A Dictionary of Liturgy and Worship.* London: SCM.

Davies, J.G. and George, A.R. (1965) *A Select Liturgical Lexicon.* London: Lutterworth.

Douglas, M. (1966) *Purity and Danger.* London: RKP.

Durkheim, E. (1961) *The Elementary Forms of the Religious Life.* (Eng. trans. J. Swain). New York: Collier.

Durston, D. (1990) 'The funeral source in the process of grieving.' *Bereavement Care 9,* 2.

Eliade, M. (1954) *The Myth of the Eternal Return.* New York: Pantheum.

Eliade, M. (1957) *Myths, Dreams and Mysteries.* London: Collins.

Eliade, M. (1958a) *Rites and Symbols of Initiation.* New York: Harper.

Eliade, M. (1958b) *Patterns of Comparative Religion.* London: Sheed & Ward.

Evans, E. Estyn (1957) *Irish Folk Ways.* London: RKP.

Evans-Pritchard, E.E., Firth R., Malinowski, B. and Schapera, I. (eds.) (1934) *Essays presented to C.G. Seligman,* London: Kegan Paul.

Evans-Wentz, W.Y. (ed) (1960) *The Tibetan Book of the Dead.* Oxford: OUP.

Fairbairn, W.R.D. (1952) *Psychoanalytic Studies of the Personality.* London: Routledge.

Festinger, L. (1957) *A Theory of Cognitive Dissonance.* Stanford University.

Fox, J. and Gill, S. (1997) *The Dead Good Funerals Book.* Ulverston, Welfare State International.

Frankfort, H. (1948) *Kingship and Gods.* Chicago: Chicago University Press.

Frankl, V.E. (1973) *Psychotherapy and Existentialism.* Harmondsworth: Penguin.

Frazer, J.G. (1933) *The Fear of the Dead in Primitive Religion.* London: Macmillan.

Freud, S. (1913) 'The theme of the three caskets' *Collected Papers Vol. 12.* London: Institute of Psychoanalysis.

Freud, S. (1914) *The Psychopathology of Everyday Life.* London: Benn.

Freud, S. (1917) *Mourning and Melancholia.* Collected Papers. Standard Edition, Vol. 14. London: Institute of Psychoanalysis.

Freud, S. (1959) *An Outline of Psychoanalysis.* Hogarth.

Geertz, C. (1966) 'Religion as a cultural system', in M. Banton (ed.), q.v. 1–46.

Gelder, K. (1994) *Reading the Vampire.* London: Routledge.

Gluckman, M. (1954) *Rituals in Rebellion of S.E. Africa.* Manchester: Manchester University Press.

Gluckman, M. (1962) *Essays in the Ritual of Social Relationships.* Manchester: Manchester University Press.

Gorer, G. (1965) *Death, Grief and Mourning in Contemporary Britain.* London: Cresset.

Gorman, C. (1972) *The Book of Ceremony.* Cambridge: Whole Earth Books.

Grainger, R. (1974) *The Language of the Rite.* London: Darton Longman & Todd.

Grainger, R. (1979) 'The social symbolism of grief and mourning.' Unpublished PhD Thesis, Leeds University.

Grainger, R. (1992) 'Diocescan chancellor rules OK.' *Contact 108.*

Habenstein, R.W. and Lamers, W.M. (1963) *Funeral Customs the World Over.* Milwaukee: Bulfin (H&L).

Hall, G. (1894) *A Manual of Christian Doctrine.* London: Longmans.

Humelin, J.-Y. (1972) 'Rélire Van Gennep: Les rites de passage.' *Maison Dieu 112.*

Harmer, R.M. (1963) *The High Cost of Dying.* New York: Crowell-Collier.

Harrington, A. (1973) *The Immortalist.* London: Panther.

Hinton, J. (1967) *Dying.* Harmondsworth: Penguin.

Hobson, R. (1970) 'My own death.' *New Blackfriars.* Vol 51, pp.469-479.

Hubert, H. and Mauss, M. (1909) *Mélanges d'Histoire des Religions.* Paris, Année Sociologique.

Ittelson, W.H. and Kilpatrick, F.P., (1964) 'Experiments in perception' in S. Coopersmith (ed.) *Frontiers of Psychological Research.* San Francisco: Freeman.

Jacobi, J. (1962) *The Psychology of C.G. Jung.* London: RKP.

James, E.O. (1958) *The Beginnings of Religion.* London: Hutchinson.

Johnson, M. (1996) in *The Dead Citizen's Charter.* Stamford: National Funerals College.

Jones, B. (1967) *Design for Death.* London: Deutsch.

Jung, C.G. (1921) 'The psychological foundations of belief in spirits', *Proceedings of the Society for Psychical Research 31,* 75–95.

Jung, C.G. (1962) 'The soul and death.' In *Collected Works,* Vol.8 (eds. H. Read, M. Fordham and G. Adler). London: Routledge.

Jung. C.G. (1981) *Man and His Symbols.* London: Aldus.

Jupp, P. (1997) 'The National Funerals College.' *Bereavement Care 16,* 2, 21.

Kastenbaum, R. and Aisenberg, R. (1974) *The Psychology of Death.* Duckworth.

Kelly, G.A. (1963) *A Theory of Personality.* New York: Norton.

Kempe, A.B. (1890) 'On the relation between the logical theory of classes and the geometric theory of points.' *Proceedings of the London Mathematical Society 21.*

Kohler, W. (1925) *The Mentality of Apes.* Harcourt.

Kubler-Ross, E. (1970) *On Death and Dying.* London: Tavistock.

Laing, R.D. (1965) *The Divided Self.* Harmondsworth: Penguin.

Layard, J. (1934) 'The journey of the dead.' in E.E. Evans-Pritchard, R. Firth, B. Malinowski and I. Schapera (eds.), q.v.

Lethbridge, C. (1967) *Ghost and Ghoul.* London: RKP.

Lewis, C.S. (1961) *A Grief Observed.* London: Faber.

Lindemann, E. (1944) 'The symptomatology and management of acute grief.' *American J. Psych 101*, pp.141–8.

Lovecraft, H.P. (1973) *Supernatural Horror in Literature*. New York: Dover.

Mackarness, R. (1974) 'Occultism and psychiatry.' *The Lancet 212*, March, 263.

Malinowski, B. (1974) *Magic, Science and Religion*. London: Souvenir Press.

Manis, M. (1966) *Cognitive Process*. Wadsworth.

Maple, E. (1964) *The Realm of Ghosts*. London: Pan.

Marcel, M. (1965) *Being and Having*. London: Collins.

Marris, P. (1958) *Widows and Their Families*. London: RKP.

Masters, A. (1974) *The Natural History of the Vampire*. London: Mayflower.

McAll, K. (1975) 'The ministry of deliverance', *The Expository Times, LXXXVI, IV: 296–298*.

McAll, K. (1982) *Healing the Family Tree*. London: SPCK.

McAll, K. (1989) *Healing the Haunted*, London: Douley Anderson.

McCabe, H. (1964) *The New Creation*. London: Sheed & Ward.

Mead, G.H. (1967) *Mind, Self and Society*. Chicago: University of Chicago.

Mitford, J. (1963) *The American Way of Death*. London: Hutchinson.

Murray, G. (1941) (Trans) *Antigone, by Sophocles*. London: Allen and Unwin.

O'Suilleabhain, S. (1967) *Irish Wake Amusements*. Cork: Mercier.

Otto, R. (1950) *The Idea of the Holy*. Oxford: OUP.

Owen, T.M. (1959) *Welsh Folk Customs*. Cardiff: National Museum of Wales.

Parkes, C.M. (1964) 'Recent bereavement as a cause of mental illness.' *Brit. J. Psychiat. 110*, p.198.

Parkes, C.M. (1965) 'Bereavement and mental illness.' *Brit. J. Med. Psychol. 38*, 1.

Parkes, C.M. (1972) *Bereavement: Studies in Grief in Adult Life*. London: Tavistock.

Perls, F.S., Hefferline, R.F. and Goodman, P. (1973) *Gestalt Therapy*. Harmondsworth: Penguin.

Pincus, L. (1976) *Death and the Family*. London: Faber.

Polson, C.J., Brittain, R.P. and Marshall, T.K. (1953) *The Disposal of the Dead*. Un. Tut. Pr.

Prim, J.G.L. (1853) *Journal of the Royal Society of Antiquaries of Ireland*. pp.330–334.

Prins, H. (1984) 'Vampirism – legendary or clinical phenomenon?' *Med. Sci. Law. 24*, 4, 283–293.

Puckle, R.S. (1926) *Funeral Customs, Their Origin & Development*. London.

Raftery, T. (ed) (1964) *The Celts*. Cork: Mercier.

Ramsay, R.W. and Happee, J.A. (1977) 'Stress of bereavement: components and treatment', in C.D. Spielberger and I.G. Sarason, q.v. pp.53–64.

Rank, O. (1958) *Beyond Psychology*. New York: Dover.

Reed, B. (1978) *The Dynamics of Religion*. London: Darton, Longman & Todd.

Richards, J. (1974) *But Deliver Us from Evil*. London: Darton, Longman & Todd.

Shropshire, D.W. (1938) *The Church and Primitive Peoples*. London: SPCK.

Spielberger, C.D. and Sarason, I.G. (1977) *Stress and Anxiety, Vol. IV*. Washington: Hemisphere.

Spranger, E. (1928) *Types of Men: the Psychology and Ethics of Personality*. (trans. P.J.W. Pigers), Halle, M. Niemayer. London.

St Clair, S. (1971) *Folklore of the Ulster People*. Cork: Mercier.

St. Victor, R. de (1959) *De Trinitate* (ed. G. Salet). Paris: Sources Chrétiennes. 63.

Sullivan, H.S. (1953) *The Interpersonal Theory of Psychiatry*. New York: Norton.

Swedenburg, (1868) *De Coeli*. London.

Tillich, P. (1952) *The Courage to Be*. London: Collins.

Toulis, R. (1995) 'Death – an Irish wake and Anglo-Saxon attitudes.' *The Guardian*, 7 October.

Turner, V.W. (1974) *The Ritual Process*. Harmondsworth: Penguin.

Vaillant, C.C. (1950) *The Aztecs of Mexico*. Harmondsworth: Penguin.

Van Gennep, A. (1965) *The Rites of Passage*. (trans: M.B. Vizedon and G.L Caffee). London: RKP.

Walter, T. (1990) *Funerals and How to Improve Them.* London: Hodder and Stoughton.

Weiner, N. (1948) *Cybernetics – or Control and Communication in the Animal and Machine.* New York: Wiley.

Weisman, A.D. (1976) 'Why is a funeral', in V. Pine et al. (eds.) *Acute Grief and the Funeral.* Thomas.

Wilde, J.F. (1971) *Ancient Legends of Ireland.* Galway: O'Gorman.

Williams, C. (1937) *Descent into Hell.* London: Faber.

Williams, H.A. (1972) *The True Resurrection.* London: Mitchell Beazley.

Wilson, M. (1975) *Health is for People.* London: Darton, Longman and Todd.

Winnicott, D.W. (1965) *The Motivational Process and the Facilitational Environment.* Hogarth Press and The Institute of Psychoanalysis.

Wretmark, A. (1993) *Perinatal Death as a Pastoral Problem.* Bibliotheca Theologiae Practicae. Stockholm: Almquist and Wiksel.

Yap, P.M. (1960) 'The possession syndrome: a comparison of Hong Kong and French findings.' *Journal of Mental Science 106.* 114–137.

Yeats, W.B. (1921) 'The Second Coming', *Michael Robartes and the Dancer.* Basingstoke: Macmillan.

Further Reading

Andrews, W. (ed) (1898) *The Church Treasury.* London: Andrews.

Bouyer, L. (1963) *Rite and Man.* London: Burns and Oates.

Chadwick, N. (1970) *The Celts.* Harmondsworth: Penguin.

Didier, J.-C. (1961) *The Last Rites.* London: Burns and Oates.

Ellis Davidson, H. (1964) *Gods and Myths of Northern Europe.* Harmondsworth: Penguin.

Hoggart, R. (1958) *The Uses of Literacy.* Harmondsworth: Penguin.

Jupp, P.C. and Howarth, G. (eds.)(1997) *The Changing Face of Death: Historical Accounts of Death and Disposal.* Basingstoke: Macmillan.

Jupp, P.C. and Rogers, T. (eds.)(1997) *Interpreting Death.* London: Cassell.

Lifton, R.J. and Olsen, E. (1974) *Living and Dying.* New York: Wildwood House.

Mason, T.H. (1967) *The Islands of Ireland.* Cork: Mercier.

Parvillez, A. (1963) *Joy in the Face of Death.* London: Faber.

Shibles, W. (1974) *Death – An Interdisciplinary Analysis.* New York: Language Press.

Walter, T. (1990) *Funerals and How to Improve them.* London: Hodder.

Walter, T. (1994) *The Revival of Death.* London: Routledge.

Young, M. and Cullen, L. (1996) *A Good Death: Conversations with East Londoners.* London: Routledge.

Editor unspecified (1973) *Folk-lore, Myths & Legends of Britain.* London: Readers' Digest Press.

INDEX